CAST
1 Peter 5:7
Richard Nilsen

All Star Press

Copyright © 2023 by Rich Nilsen

All rights reserved. No part of this book may be used; reproduced, or transmitted in any manner whatsoever without permission in writing from the publisher or author except in the case of brief quotations embodied in critical articles and reviews.

Published by All Star Press - Books that Change Lives

Tarpon Springs, Florida

Edited by Shannon Gale, Samantha Schafer

First edition: November 2023

ISBN # 978-1-937376-44-4

Library of Congress number: 2023945993

What Others Are Saying
Testimonials for CAST

"Thank you for sharing your beautifully written book, CAST, with me. This amazing book has helped me to enrich my understanding of the Bible and helped give me focus to see God's Word more clearly through all the stories and examples you wrote. Growing in God's Word is allowing us all to grow in our Love for Him! So, books like this are very important to us all to strengthen our walk with our Lord and Savior Jesus Christ! God is Great!"

~ Rudy Shaffer, Water4Life Ministry

"Richard Nilsen, the author of CAST, offers some valuable suggestions for living a peaceful life by weaving together some biblical references as well as stories of both well-known and average people. He also uses examples from his own life experiences as he lays out some simple steps for achieving trust in a loving God. This book is well worth reading; perhaps more than once!"

~ Denise Crompton, Author of 'Diagnosis: Rare Disease'

"Worth the read! I highly recommend Nilsen's book, CAST.

As a bereaved mom, I am reminding myself to cast my hurt onto the Lord. I have learned throughout the years that only Christ gives me a peace that surpasses all understanding."

~ Sheryl Crosier, Author of 'I Am Not A Syndrome - My Name is Simon'

"We love the heart behind your new book [CAST], and it is certainly a timely message for our world today - to cast our cares on the One who cares for us. I pray it blesses and encourages everyone who reads it. May God bless you."

~ Samaritan's Purse, Boone, NC

"Loved, loved, loved the book! I guess I'm going fishing soon.... maybe tonight!! I know for sure I will CAST my net tonight!!

"Nilsen's writing connected with so much that I have going on in my life right now. I have so many miracles and blessings in my life, but there is a lot of debris in the path currently. I'm in a major struggle right now and I need to CAST it out to God. I know He's got this. Starting my 'Gratitude Journal' today."

~ Gerard Ramos, Louisana businessman

"This is what I call meat and potatoes kind of biblical teaching. I really like the practical steps and application Nilsen suggests applying at the end of each chapter, too. This is a book I can tell will need to be read several times. It is written so comprehensible for any level of believer or non believer to understand. I cried a lot. It is so good! And I already have many people in mind that I'm going to recommend purchasing your book. This truly is a book for everyone to read!"

~ Christina Blackmon, Florida mom

"I loved CAST. The stories that are told throughout brought back a few memories of my own. I must say thank you for giving me the idea of starting my own journal. Many times in my life I can see where God had his hand in it. I sometimes wondered how I would make it through. With trust in God I did each time, and I am realizing it more and more.

I also love how you have illustrated the casting of your cares to God. You have to believe that God will handle your problems and concerns. I have been practicing on giving all my cares to God for a while now and I am getting better at it. Life is getting better. Great book!"

~ Nina Carothers, author of 'The Color Olors Series'

Contents

Dedication	IX
1. He Lived Among ISIS Yet Slept in Peace	1
2. Definition of Casting	5
3. Our Will Be Done	11
4. Faith in Action	17
5. How to Cast Our Cares to the Lord	25
6. Biblical Guidance for Casting Our Cares to God	47
7. Experience is the Teacher	55
8. Control Your Intake	65
9. The Freedom of the Son	69
10. Some of Our Cares?	75
11. His Eyes Are on the Sparrow	81
12. A Treasure Trove of Blessings	85
13. Real World Examples	91
14. The Creator – Evidence	111
Addendum	117

Addendum 2	139
Acknowledgments	144
About the Author	147
Also By Richard Nilsen	148
References	151

I dedicate this book to my three beautiful daughters – Paradise, Genesis and Natalie. I pray that they will apply the Biblical principles of 1 Peter 5:7 into their daily lives, and that they will let the Creator of the universe handle their problems for them.

Chapter One

He Lived Among ISIS Yet Slept in Peace

"Cast your cares on the Lord and he will sustain you;he will never let the righteous be shaken." Psalm 55:22 (NIV)

Petr Jasek is a Christian missionary who has traveled around the world, helping the less fortunate in the name of Jesus Christ. He has taught the Gospel to people who might otherwise never hear God's word, and he has helped countless souls come to Christ. His amazing story is told in the book, "Imprisoned with ISIS: Faith in the Face of Evil." [1]

Over the years, one of his international destinations was Sudan. Sudan is a country with a corrupt government in the northeast part of Africa, just south of Egypt and Libya, and Muslims make up an estimated 97% of the population. For three long decades (1989 – 2019) Sudan experienced a military dictatorship led by a tyrant named Omar al-Bashir. He was accused of widespread human-rights abuses including torture, persecution of minorities, and ethnic genocide. During al-Bashir's horrific regime, the entire legal system in Sudan was based on Islamic Sharia law. Legal forms of punishment included stoning, flogging, and crucifixion.

In 2017, Petr was on one of his mission trips to the war-torn country with the objective of meeting up with fellow Christians. As he was about to depart for home, he was accosted at the airport and brought to an interrogation room. What Petr thought would be a routine question-and-answer session suddenly turned into a nightmare. He was being arrested as a spy.

Petr soon found himself in a Sudanese prison. The conditions of the prison were beyond deplorable. Sometimes, Petr would be freezing cold with access to only one filthy blanket. Other times, he and the other prisoners would be subjected to heat exceeding 110 degrees; and to make matters worse, this was coupled with limited water supply. The prison cells were built to accommodate three to four prisoners, but the authorities would pack 15, 20, or more captives into one small room.

In one prison where he resided for over a year, the water would only come on for a brief period each day. Brown, murky water would come out of the pipes, and prisoners like Petr would have to attempt to filter it to make it somewhat acceptable to use.

The majority of the time Petr was treated very poorly by both his Islamic cellmates and the prison guards. He was regularly beaten by his cellmates, who considered him an infidel. It did not take long before he discovered that many of his fellow prisoners were members of Islamic State of Iraq and Syria (ISIS).

Petr was held captive at the time of the 2017 Paris bombings. When his cellmates learned of the horrific attacks, they erupted into huge cheers. The chanting of "ala akbur" sent shivers down his spine.

Shortly after he was arrested as a prisoner, Petr thought that he would be released fairly quickly. At times, the prison guards would even trick him into thinking that he would be released. The mental challenges were as great as the physical challenges.

Weeks became months, and months turned into years. After some time and having been moved around to multiple prison locations, Petr realized that he was beginning to impact the lives of some prisoners. He found ways to use the time in prison to minister to others and to share the Gospel of Christ. The impact was great, and Petr felt that the Lord was indeed using him to move His kingdom forward.

Despite some of these positive outcomes, Petr was still surviving every day under horrific circumstances. One of the most inconceivable things he had to endure was sleeping on hard, cold floors with little to no covering. For those of us who sleep in a comfortable bed each evening, along with air conditioning or heat to make the room the perfect temperature, the thought of sleeping in bitterly cold or obnoxiously hot temperatures on a rock-hard surface with filthy bed sheets is beyond our comprehension.

However, Petr Jasek slept like a baby nearly every night during his capture. How is that even remotely possible? We'll come back to that.

CAST

Chapter Two
Definition of Casting

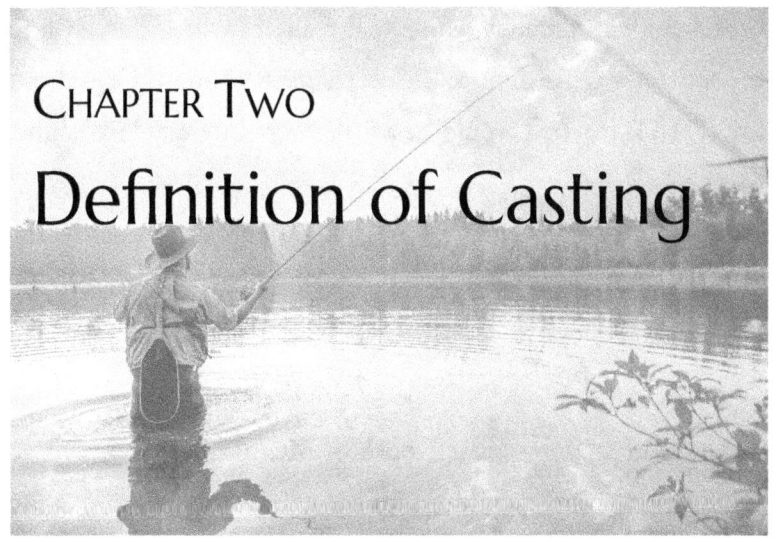

I am not a fisherman. As a child, I went fishing with my dad several times, so I learned some of the basics – setting up the bait, casting the line, and waiting. Lots of waiting.

Later in life, after I married my wife Marta, I again went fishing on several occasions. Many of these times was with my in-laws. Like my own dad, my father-in-law Carl and mother-in-law Patty also enjoyed fishing. They would often take their bass boat from the mountains of North Carolina to Norris Lake or Watauga Lake in Tennessee. Both lakes were beautiful spots for their favorite pastime.

As popular as the sport is, fishing has never been my thing. It's probably because I lacked patience, and I thoroughly enjoyed participating in sports that had a lot of action. If I wanted trout, I'd go buy it at Kroger or Publix.

Despite my lack of passion for fishing, I could recognize a good fisherman when I saw one. In my opinion, the first sign of a good fisherman was someone who could really cast their line far into the spot they wanted. Into the deep waters. Now, if I could cast like THAT, maybe I would be a little more interested in fishing. Maybe.

The Word Cast and Its Depth of Meaning

There are several definitions for the word 'cast' – from 'causing a light or shadow to appear on a surface' to 'registering a vote.' However, one of the more popular definitions is "throwing the hooked and baited end of a fishing line into the water."

Another more general definition is "to throw something forcefully in a specific direction." In fact, the origin of the word comes from Old English circa 1200s. According to the Online Etymonline Dictionary, the verb cast means "to throw, throw violently, fling, hurl."

The word cast has a lot of applications. It can be used as a noun. A cast may refer to "an object made by shaping molten metal or similar material in a mold." It can also be the "act of throwing something forcefully." Queue the fishing images.

Of course, cast can also be referring to the collection of characters in a movie or TV show.

Two other lesser-known definitions include "the form or appearance of something, especially someone's features or complexion" or "a slight squint."

"Cast" can also be a part of other words. Think of outcast. An outcast is someone who has been "thrown out" of their society. Probably the most well-known outcasts in the Biblical stories are lepers. People with the disease of leprosy were rejected and forced to live outside the perimeter of the city. No one would dare go near a leper, so when Jesus not only touched but also healed some leapers, it created quite a stir.

The Intricacies of Casting a Fishing Line

When I hear the word cast, I immediately draw up the imagery of a fisherman. It may be the fly fisherman who is casting his line in the river as the majestic Grand Tetons tower in the background. Or it may be the local fishermen who cast their lines into the Gulf of Mexico off the Fred Howard causeway, a beautiful spot near my house in Florida.

Maybe you have a specific recollection of a fisherman who could really cast their line, and that is the imagery you bring up when you hear the word.

Like any other sport, excelling at a specific skill requires both practice and knowledge.

Fishing expert and writer Jason Sealock says that there are eight factors[1] that affect the casting of a line:

- Rod action
- Rod length
- Line size
- Line material
- Lure weight
- Lure shape or size
- Wind
- Lure-to-rod tip distance

"Every one of these factors affects your ability to cast the lure where you want to," says Sealock, who goes on to explain how each determines the fisherman's success, or lack thereof.

He compares the action of the rod to that of a slingshot. The harder you can pull it back, the farther it can propel the item (in this case, the lure). However, the quality of the fishing rod (the tool) plays a factor in this, too.

In addition, the length of the rod can determine how far the line can be thrown. In general, a longer fishing rod produces a longer cast than a shorter rod with a fisherman employing the same force and action. Each type of fishing rod has a limit to how much weight it can cast effectively.

Sealock goes on to explain that a thinner fishing line will cast better than a bulkier or thicker line. It's all about drag.

"Thickness plays a role, and so can the coating and material of the line," explains Sealock. "A 30-pound braid throws a lot farther than a 20-pound fluorocarbon does...so, the lure can actually pull the line off the reel with less effort and friction on a cast."

It doesn't end there. The weight of the lure plays a major factor. A 1-ounce lure has a better chance for a long cast than a ½-oz lure. However, that can change if the 1-oz. lure is not aerodynamic. Not surprisingly, the shape and design of the lure can affect distance.

If you have the wind at your back when casting, your chances for a nice cast improve. You don't have to be a rocket scientist to know that if you are casting into a headwind or crosswind, this might not work out quite as well...especially if you are not skilled at casting.

Finally, before you cast, ensure that too much fishing line does not hang out from the tip of the rod. The right length will vary according to the rig (combination of hooks, sinkers, snaps, and swivels), rod length, and casting style used, but a recommendation for novices is to use one quarter of the rod length. Limiting the length of the line will allow the momentum of the cast to kick in sooner, resulting in more distance relative to the effort.

After researching the art of casting, I now know why I am not good at casting! It's complicated, and like any other sport, it requires skill and lots of practice.

Learning to fish is not easy, and neither is learning to cast your cares to God. However, with some knowledge and a little practice, you will soon have the confidence to cast in a way that reaps rewards.

Even Moses had to learn this skill and it only took him four decades.

Chapter Three
Our Will Be Done

A well-known Biblical story is found in the Book of Exodus. As a baby, Moses was put in a basket and floated down the river, where he was discovered by the Pharaoh's daughter and her servants. Moses was taken in by the Pharaoh's daughter and raised as one of her children in the Egyptian kingdom.

Years later, Moses would witness an injustice and recklessly take matters into his own hands.

"One day, after Moses had grown up, he went out to where his own people were and watched them at their hard labor. He saw an Egyptian beating a Hebrew, one of his own people. Looking this way and that and seeing no one, he killed the Egyptian and hid him in the sand. The next day he went out and saw two Hebrews fighting. He asked the one in the wrong, 'Why are you hitting your fellow Hebrew?'

The man said, 'Who made you ruler and judge over us? Are you thinking of killing me as you killed the Egyptian?' Then Moses was afraid and thought, 'What I did must have become known.'

When Pharaoh heard of this, he tried to kill Moses, but Moses fled from Pharaoh and went to live in Midian..."[1]

As a child in Pharaoh's palace, Moses would have witnessed many injustices. Surely this was not the first time that Moses had seen abuse and slavery. However, something about this particular incident caused Moses to lose control and commit murder. If that wasn't bad enough, he attempted to cover up his crime and proceed as if life was normal. It only took a single day before he realized the gig was up and his crime was not a secret.

How often are you just like Moses? You see something you adamantly disagree with or that upsets you, and instead of casting your cares to God, you take matters into your own hands.

Gossip. Fire back that text. Snap back with the quick insult. Be a keyboard warrior on social media. Lift a finger to that driver who cut you off in traffic. The list is endless.

Just like you, Moses had a choice: release his cares into God's hands and trust Him, or attempt to 'solve' the problem for himself. Moses, of course, chose the latter and the result was life changing.

The Pharaoh sent a team to track down Moses and kill him. Soon, Moses was on the run and he would spend 40 years in the desert (see Acts 7:30). It would take that long before God would allow him to participate in the historic task of freeing his people.

After spending those four decades in Midian, Moses learned to transition from a spoiled member of the royal family, who only knew life in the palace, to the shepherd life in the wilderness. Moses learned patience, humility, gratitude and trust for his Maker, for whom he held a deep reverence.

At the appointed time, God called for Moses, taking the form of a burning bush. God spelled out his instructions to Moses, but it didn't take long for him to object and come up with various excuses.

"But suppose they will not believe me, nor listen to my plea? For they may say, 'The Lord did not appear to you.'"[2]

God proceeded to perform multiple miracles in Moses' sight. But that didn't stop Moses from continuing to voice his objection.

"I have never been eloquent, neither in the past, nor recently. Nor now that you have spoken to your servant, but I am slow of speech and tongue."[3]

God had an answer for Moses' excuses. He explained to Moses that he can utilize his brother Aaron's speaking abilities and have him talk on his behalf to the Israelites.

It is easy to see yourself in Moses. Despite witnessing multiple blessings and miracles, you may continue to doubt God. You may continue to make excuses as to why you are not able to perform a task that the Lord has called you to do.

Instead of leaning on his own power and decision-making, Moses became obedient to his Lord. In the end God delivered the Israelites from Egypt in dramatic fashion.

Moses led his people into the desert, on God's orders, but his challenges were far from over. He quickly faced the wrath of the followers.

The people complained to Moses, "Was it because there were no graves in Egypt that you brought us to the desert to die? What have you done to us by bringing us out of Egypt? Didn't we say to you in Egypt, 'Leave us alone; let us serve the Egyptians?' It would have been better for us to serve the Egyptians than to die in the desert!"[4]

By then, Moses had developed complete confidence in God. He no longer took matters into his own hands. He no longer let emotions control him. He now relied 100 percent on instructions from his Lord and did so with confidence.

Moses answered the people, "Do not be afraid. Stand firm and you will see the deliverance the Lord will bring you today. The Egyptians you see today you will never see again. The Lord will fight for you; you need only to be still."[5]

Then the angel of God, who had been traveling in front of Israel's army, withdrew and went behind them. The pillar of cloud also moved from in front and stood behind them, coming between the armies of Egypt and Israel. Throughout the night the cloud brought darkness to the one side and light to the other side; so neither went near the other all night long.

Then Moses stretched out his hand over the sea, and all that night the Lord drove the sea back with a strong east wind and turned it into dry land. The waters were divided, and the Israelites went through the sea on dry ground, with a wall of water on their right and on their left.

The Egyptians pursued them, and all Pharaoh's horses and chariots and horsemen followed them into the sea. During the last watch of the night the Lord looked down from the pillar of fire and cloud at the Egyptian army and threw it into confusion. He jammed the wheels of their chariots so that they had difficulty driving. And the Egyptians said, "Let's get away from the Israelites! The Lord is fighting for them against Egypt."

Then the Lord said to Moses, "Stretch out your hand over the sea so that the waters may flow back over the Egyptians and their chariots and horsemen." Moses stretched out his hand over the sea, and at daybreak the sea went back to its place. The Egyptians were fleeing toward it, and the Lord swept them into the sea. The water flowed back and covered the chariots and horsemen—the entire army of Pharaoh that had followed the Israelites into the sea. Not one of them survived.

But the Israelites went through the sea on dry ground, with a wall of water on their right and on their left. That day the Lord saved Israel from the hands of the Egyptians, and Israel saw the Egyptians lying dead on the shore. And when the Israelites saw the mighty hand of the Lord displayed against the Egyptians, the people feared the Lord and put their trust in him and in Moses his servant. [6]

His Will Be Done

If you can be like younger Moses who lacked discipline, acted on impulse, and relied on his own knowledge and decision-making 'skills,' then you can also be like the older, wiser Moses. The same Moses who confronted the Egyptian Pharoah. The same Moses who delivered the Israelites to freedom.

How do you transform and grow and begin acting like the wiser Moses, who knew how to cast his cares?

You obey.

You seek God's counsel first.

You surrender your will to God.

You focus on God and not the problem.

You act with confidence.

You don't let distractors get you off course.

Action Items

Take deliberate steps to be like the older, wiser Moses. Find one problem this week that you can leave in God's hands.

Chapter Four
Faith in Action

"There is no fear in love, but perfect love casts out fear...whoever fears has not been perfected in love." ~ 1 John 4:18 (ESV)

In 1824, Charles Blondin of France trained to be an acrobat and tightrope walker, and he soon became known as the "Boy Wonder" as he performed in front of audiences as early as age five. At the age of 31, he took his show to the United States where he performed many daring acts on the high wire.

Blondin's work led to great fame throughout the world. He became so well known that presidential candidate Abraham Lincoln compared himself to "Blondin on the tightrope, with all that was valuable to America in the wheelbarrow he was pushing before him."

Lincoln was referring to Blondin's most famous act: walking across Niagara Falls numerous times, including instances in which he pushed a wheelbarrow.

Abraham Lincoln depicted as Charles Blondin.(1)

On July 15, 1859, Blondin dazzled his audiences by going back and forth across Niagara Falls. The massive waters raged below the quarter-mile span of wire. Blondin awed the crowds with his death-defying performances that day. He did it blindfolded. He did it on stilts. He did it carrying a man on his back. As the story goes, he crossed over to the Canadian side where he was met with tremendous applause. He then took a wheelbarrow and pushed it back across the wire to the United States side. Again, Blondin was met with accolades from the admiring fans. There was no shortage of praise being thrown at Charles Blondin.

He asked the crowd if they believed he could push a person in the wheelbarrow across the wire, and people in the crowd responded affirmatively. The cheers grew and the crowd continued to shout words of praise and admiration.

Blondin then asked for anyone in the crowd to join him by sitting in the wheelbarrow as he pushed it back to the Canadian side. The crowd grew silent. Before them was the greatest high wire act in the world, but Blondin had no takers.

Get in the wheelbarrow? No thanks!

My dad used to insist that "talk is cheap." Of all the fans unloading their praise on to the great French acrobat, not a single person would get in the wheelbarrow. They were content sitting on the sidelines and watching his amazing feats from a distance.

Aren't we just like that, all too often? It is easy to talk a good game, but ask me to put on football equipment and get hit by a 280lb linebacker? I'll pass. Let someone else do the hard work. Let someone else take the risk.

Faith is about taking action and casting our cares and worries to the Lord.

Removing Back-up Plans

There is another story about a man taking bold action. In February 1519, conquistador Hernán Cortés arrived from Spain in the New World with his men, and he soon realized that he would have to conquer the Aztec Empire.[2] His men were not focused and they kept one eye on their escape plan: the boats. Cortés realized that he had to eliminate their escape option. His men had to be forced to face their fears and win at all costs. Cortés would not let them have the choice of retreating and returning to their old lives.

Cortés ordered his men to take all their supplies off the boats and disembark. According to historians, he then proceeded to have the boats burned or scuttled. Whether it was by fire or by sinking, the boats were gone. Cortés had cast their backup plans into the depths of the ocean.

His men were now forced to focus on one goal, settling here on the land that they had discovered. There was no Plan B, no turning back.

Cortés had faith that he and his men could win the battle. He had faith that if his men were focused and had no other alternatives, they would accomplish their mission. And they did.

Hernán Cortés and his men defeated the Aztec Empire, and the conquistador became a legend in the process. He was appointed Governor of New Spain in 1522 by King Charles I.

Put Me in Coach

If you are currently sitting on the sidelines, then you need to put your faith into action. Sitting on the bench and watching others play is no way to be a teammate, and certainly no way of demonstrating faith and trust in God.

In the 1980s, musician John Fogarty had a great song entitled "Centerfield," or also known as "Put Me in Coach."

Fogarty's well-known lyrics[3] read:

Well, beat the drum and hold the phone - the sun came out today!
We're born again, there's new grass on the field.
A-roundin' third, and headed for home, it's a brown-eyed handsome man;
Anyone can understand the way I feel.
Chorus:
Oh, put me in, Coach - I'm ready to play today;
Put me in, Coach - I'm ready to play today;
Look at me, I can be Centerfield.

God doesn't want you riding the bench. He wants you in the game. The Lord reminds you in the second chapter of James that "faith by itself, if it does not result in action, is dead."[4]

If Cortés' men had just remained on the boats and watched from the safe distance of the shore, they would not have changed the world. Instead, they got out of the boats and sprang into action. To make sure that they would remain persistent and diligent, Cortés, their leader, had to first remove the option of escape. He scuttled the ships, and the rest is history.

Moses spent four decades in the desert learning the attributes that the Lord wanted him to possess. When the time was ready,

God called for him to take action. Moses responded and, in the end, became one of the most influential men in the history of the world.

In baseball, centerfield is considered the key fielding position. The player put in the centerfield position is the leader of the outfield and, often times, the best fielder with the best arm. You don't have to be the centerfielder on God's baseball team, but you do need to be in the game. If you are just riding the bench, watching everyone else participate, then you are not contributing your God-given ability. Every player position on a baseball team is important, whether it's a relief pitcher or the first baseman.

Action Items

Think about your unique skills. How can you put those skills into action and glorify God?

Look for one area in your life where you are 'sitting on the sidelines' and not in the game. Choose one step this week where you can get in the game.

CAST

Chapter Five
How to Cast Our Cares to the Lord

"Come to me, all you who are weary and burdened, and I will give you rest. Take my yoke upon you and learn from me, for I am gentle and humble in heart, and you will find rest for your souls." ~ Matthew 11:28-29 (NIV)

In reading this book and putting the advice into practice, you will learn how to cast your cares to the Lord. To lighten your burdens and strengthen your faith, you need to throw your concerns to God. When doing so, you let the Creator of the universe become your earthly father. Fathers on earth are there to nurture, raise and guide their children. They are also there to protect their children and help them with their burdens.

Struggles oftentimes vary in complexity, so it is not always easy to surrender and cast your cares but it is worth the effort. There are a few vital steps to doing this successfully. Let's lean in.

Step One: Acceptance

For starters, you need to acknowledge Jesus Christ as Lord and Savior of your life. Without that acknowledgment, any casting of your cares is nearly impossible. If you do not believe in Him, how could you possibly give your problems to Him?

Let's address Jesus' role in your life. Jesus is called Lord for a reason. A lord rules over everything and everyone. He controls all. He masters all. He reigns over His own kingdom. A Lord is the supreme ruler; therefore, Jesus is the supreme ruler of your life if you believe in Him.

> "Therefore God highly exalted Him, and bestowed on Him the name which is above every name, that at the name of Jesus every knee should bow, in heaven, and on the earth, and under the earth, and every tongue confess that Jesus Christ is Lord, to the glory of God the Father." ~ Philippians 2:9-11 (ESV)

If you haven't accepted Him, invite God into your heart. It's not complicated. Just do it.

As a Christian, you know who your Lord is. You have to believe and trust Him. In 1 Peter 2:9, we are told that we are "a chosen people, a royal priesthood...a people for God's own possession."[1] With that understanding, it is time to take your problems to your Father in Heaven.

> *"Yes, leave it with Him,*
> *The lilies all do,*
> *And they grow –*
> *And they grow in the dew –*
> *Yes, they grow:*
> *They grow in the darkness, all hid in the night –*
> *They grow in the sunshine, revealed by the light –*
> *Still they grow.*
> *Yes, leave it to Him,*
> *It's more dear to His heart,*
> *You will know,*
> *Than the lilies that bloom,*
> *Or the flowers that start,*
> *'Neath the snow:*
> *Whatever you need, if you seek it in prayer,*
> *You can leave it with Him – for you are His care,*
> *You, you know.* ~ Streams In The Desert

Step Two: Define the Problem and Fling It

You need to recognize exactly what it is that is bothering you. Is it anger? Are you worried about something in particular? Has someone offended you? You need to be fully honest about the issue or issues at hand. For example, stating that I am mad at my brother doesn't really cut it. Stating that I'm hurt deeply by his specific actions and that I need to forgive him gets more to the heart of the issue. Be specific.

Maybe you don't know how to forgive that person and just feel that it is an impossible task. That is the perfect time to ask for His help. You could pray, "Lord, I don't know if I can forgive my brother...or if I even want to. I don't know how to do this, but my ill will towards him is eating me up. This anger is negatively affecting my life and the lives of those around me. Take this from me. Show me what I need to do."

In Mark, Chapter 11, Jesus tells his disciples: "Truly I tell you, if anyone says to this mountain, 'Go, throw yourself into the sea,' and does not doubt in their heart but believes that what they say will happen, it will be done for them."[2]

'This' mountain is very specific. Jesus wants us to address the precise problem, not the entire mountain range.

Surrender your negative thoughts to the Lord. Speak it out loud. In Jeremiah 29:12, you are told that if you call upon the Lord, He will listen to you. That is the promise you can hold on to firmly.

"Lord, I can't handle this issue. I am giving You my anger. I am giving You my hurt and pain over this situation with my _____."

When you throw your cares to the Lord, you re-direct your focus off the problem and on to your Creator. This immediately changes your perspective, which is very helpful when you are worried or anxious about a problem. Casting your cares takes your focus off your own inability and weaknesses and puts the focus on the One who can take care of the problem.

You should immediately feel some sense of peace if you have truly cast your problem(s) to the Lord. It does not mean the hurt or suffering has suddenly gone away, but it does mean that you have turned your cares over to Him, and you no longer carry the full weight of the burden.

When you fail to do this, you can end up obsessing over whatever the problem is during this time in your life. When you obsess, you turn the problem or situation over and over in your mind. This results in trying to solve the issue on your end. Oftentimes, that is a complete waste of time or leads to consequences you did not intend.

Pray for a clear head. Recognize what the problem is. Fling your cares to the Creator of the universe and let Him handle them.

Step Three: Trust Him to Honor His Promises

> "I write these things to you who believe in the name of the Son of God so that you may know that you have eternal life. **This is the confidence you have in approaching God: that if you ask anything according to his will, he hears you.**" ~ 1 John 5:13-14 (NIV)

Believe with 100 percent certainty that He will accept your cares and handle them for you. You have to believe this. Besides, why should you doubt? You are talking about the creator of the universe, the stars and all the incredible sights and sounds that you have witnessed throughout your life. The proof of God's existence is all around you.

Just like children often have to trust their parents, you need to trust God. Children don't always understand why their mom or dad asks them to follow instructions. The child just realizes that his or her parents know better and understand what is good for them. An obedient child – a wise child – trusts his or her parent even when they don't understand.

In his book *"Enthusiasm Makes the Difference,"* the inspirational writer and minister Norman Vincent Peale told the story of a woman he met at a luncheon in Chicago.

The young lady, dressed in a waitress outfit and roughly 30 years of age, raced up to Dr. Peale at the conclusion of his speech and announced, "Dr. Peale, I just love you!" She went on to tell him about her difficult situation which included abandonment by the father of her child. Despite the desertion, this mother was happy to have a wonderful son. Unfortunately, at the age of five, the boy became very sick.

The child's physician told her, "Mary, you've got to be strong. I don't know whether we can save your boy or not." She was distraught and could see her entire world falling apart.

Then she explained to Dr. Peale that a neighbor gave her one of his sermons. In it, Peale had stated, "If you have a loved one who is ill or about whom you are worried, don't hold this loved one too closely. Give the loved one to God. God gave him [or her] to you. He isn't yours, really; he is God's. So, give him to God, for God is good, He is loving, He is a great kind Father who holds each child in His love. Let go and let God care for him. No harm, only good can come to him when he is in God's hands."

She had never heard any advice like this before but decided to cast her immense worries to the Lord and place them into His hands, fully trusting in Him. "It seemed awfully hard to do," explained Mary. "But something inside my heart told me that it was right. So, I prayed like you said and I put my boy in God's hands."

She demonstrated how she lifted her hands up to God as if raising a child to Him.

Smiling through tears of joy, Mary pined, "Isn't God good? He let me keep my boy. And now God and I are raising him together."[3]

James 1:6 says to simply believe because those who doubt are "like a wave of the seas, blown and tossed by the wind."[4]

The Holy Bible tells you to give your problems to the Lord. If God's Word instructs you to do this, then why should you have any doubt?

> "Now to him who is able to do immeasurably more than all we ask or imagine, according to his power that is at work within us, to him be glory in the church and in Christ Jesus throughout all generations, for ever and ever! Amen." ~ Ephesians 3:20-21 (NIV)

The well-known Old Testament story of the Israelites and the land of Canaan highlights this lesson. God ordered Moses to assign one person to represent each of the 12 tribes of Israel and have them go scope out the land He promised them and come back with a report.

After spending 40 days in the land of Canaan, the 12 spies returned with their report for Aaron and Moses.

"They gave Moses this account: 'We went into the land to which you sent us, and it does flow with milk and honey! Here is its fruit. **But** *the people who live there are powerful,* **and** *the cities are fortified and very large.* **We even** *saw descendants of Anak there. The*

Amalekites live in the Negev; the Hittites, Jebusites and Amorites live in the hill country; and the Canaanites live near the sea and along the Jordan."

Then Caleb silenced the people before Moses and said, 'We should go up and take possession of the land, for we can certainly do it.'

*But the men who had gone up with him said, '**We can't** attack those people; they are **stronger than we are**.' And they spread among the Israelites a bad report about the land they had explored. They said, 'The land we explored **devours** those living in it. All the people we saw there are of great size. We saw the Nephilim there (the descendants of Anak come from the Nephilim). We seemed like grasshoppers in our own eyes, and we looked the same to them.' "*[5]

Fear. Fear. And more fear. Caleb and Joshua stood strong in their faith, but the other 10 leaders spread a message of fear. **But. And. We even...We can't. They are stronger.** As the report continued, their trepidation became even more exaggerated, as the residents of Canaan became like giants in their imaginations. By the time the report was finished, the Canaanites were an insurmountable foe.

The Israelites chose comfort over relying on the promise of God. Instead of casting their fears aside, they gave into fear.

The English poet and hymnwriter Frances Ridley Havergal says, "Every year I live – in fact, every day – I seem to see more clearly how all the peace, happiness and power of the Christian life hinges on one thing. <u>That one thing is taking God on His word</u>, believing that He really means exactly what He says, and accepting the very words that reveal His goodness and grace, without substituting other words or changing the precise moods and tenses He has seen fit to use."[6]

The success of the Christian life hinges on taking God at His word. There is no reason to doubt God. "That one thing" that gives power to your Christian life is taking God on His word. You have a role in God carrying out his plans. Your faith says to accept Him on His word. As Havergal states, you will be at peace when you take God at His word. You will enjoy more happiness, and you will experience the power of the Christian life.

In addition, there are many times when you want to dictate to God how He should answer your prayers. You submit the prayer request along with the question and answer. *This is how I want You to answer my prayer, Lord. Please get it done for me.*

You may want things to go a certain way, but that is not how it works. When you trust in your Creator, you also have to trust that He knows what is the best outcome. He knows how things will work best for those who love Him. Although easier said than done, you have to trust that He knows better than you.

Step Four: Be Thankful

Thank Him for taking on your cares and relieving you of the burden.

"Do not be anxious about anything, but in every situation, by prayer and petition, with **thanksgiving**, present your requests to God. And the peace of God, which transcends all understanding, will guard your hearts and your minds in Christ Jesus." ~ Philippians 4:6-7 (NIV)

You have cast your cares onto the Lord; they are now His to handle. It is time to be thankful.

Jesus sets the example of gratitude. In John, Chapter 11, Jesus looked up to heaven and said, "Father, I thank you that you have heard me. I knew that you always hear me, but I said this on account of the people standing around, that they may believe that you sent me."[7] So, what happens next? Lazarus, who has been dead for three days, responds to Jesus' call to come out and he exits the tomb to the bewilderment of the many witnesses. Jesus set the example of thanking his Father in Heaven just prior to the answer.

Unlike the novice fisherman who feels a slight tug on the line and impatiently reels in the line to see what is going on, you need to cast and let it go. Casting is an act of trust. You trust God that He will handle your issue. Thank Him.

The famous poet Ralph Waldo Emerson penned the following well known poem:

We Thank Thee
By Ralph Waldo Emerson

For flowers that bloom about our feet,
Father, we thank Thee.
For tender grass so fresh, so sweet,
Father, we thank Thee.
For the song of bird and hum of bee,
For all things fair we hear or see,
Father in heaven, we thank Thee.
For blue of stream and blue of sky,
Father, we thank Thee.
For pleasant shade of branches high,
Father, we thank Thee.
For fragrant air and cooling breeze,
For beauty of the blooming trees,
Father in heaven, we thank Thee.
For this new morning with its light,
Father, we thank Thee.
For rest and shelter of the night,
Father, we thank Thee
For health and food, for love and friends,
For everything Thy goodness sends,
Father in heaven, we thank Thee.

Step Five: Abide in Christ

You may be familiar with the story of Mary and Martha, found in Chapter 10 of the Book of Luke. Jesus has been traveling and has arrived at the home of the two sisters. In this story, it is pretty clear that Martha is stressed out about Jesus' arrival. When He arrives, Martha is still working diligently around the house, tidying up, cleaning, and preparing meals. Meanwhile, her sister Mary is not doing any of those things. Instead, she sits at the feet of Jesus and listens intently to what the Savior is saying. Maybe Mary got her work done early and had margin in her life, while her sister had procrastinated. Who knows.

Mary is sitting at Jesus' feet, listening to His every word, and anxious Martha finally has had enough. She loses her composure. She complains about the frustrating situation to Jesus and asks Him to force Mary to help her.

Jesus replies, "Martha, Martha, you are worried and upset about many things, but only one thing is needed. Mary has chosen what is better, and it will not be taken away from her."[8]

Mary and Martha are both given the same opportunity – to abide in Jesus. However, only one of them chooses wisely. The other thinks that she is doing the right thing by continuing to work around the house, but in fact, Martha has chosen very poorly. Instead of spending the precious time with Jesus, she is frantically working on things that only matter on the surface and not eternally.

I have lost track of how many times I have acted like Martha.

The scenarios are endless. Every time that I have chosen to mindlessly surf the internet instead of spending time in God's Word is a Martha decision. Every time that I have taken a selfish action instead of utilizing that time to help others is a Martha decision. When I have chosen myself over my children, that is a Martha decision.

Don't be like Martha. Choose to abide in Jesus.

Every time that you choose wisely, it becomes easier to cast your cares onto Him. When you are in close relationship with your Lord, it is easier to communicate with Him. How can you cast your cares onto someone you don't know? It's possible, of course, but significantly harder.

Late in the book of Matthew, Jesus answered the question of the Saducees by telling them that they were misled "because [they] did not know the scriptures or the power of God."[9]

You don't want to be among those who are misled. You want to be on the side of those with wisdom and knowledge. That is accomplished by abiding in Him.

> "Seek the Lord and his strength; seek his presence continually!" ~ Psalm 105:4 (ESV)

Author Jim George tells the story of when he was a future seminary student and was new to the Christian faith. A man came to speak at church, and George was very impressed with the man's knowledge of the Bible.

George summoned up the courage to talk to the man after he was done speaking and enquired of the man how he knew the Bible so well. He didn't get the answer he expected. George expected the man to refer to his theological training or his God-given ability to interpret the scriptures. However, he replied that it was simply a result of daily reading the Bible over the course of his lifetime.[10]

It was not complicated. This man had spent many decades regularly reading and taking in God's word. He was consistent and loyal to that task.

In college, I was told by one professor that if you read up on a particular subject every day for five years, you will become an expert in that field. Some of you have done this in whatever field, sport, or hobby is of interest to you, and as a result, you know it pretty darn well. What if you did the same with God's word?

By consistently diving into the Old Testament and New Testament on a daily basis, you begin to know God's heart and you learn to trust Him more. You learn the instructions for your life that He has laid out for you in the Holy Bible. This nourishes you spiritually the same way that food and water nourish you physically.

By reading His word daily, you begin to see how personal scripture is meaningful to you and your family. You begin to see and recognize all the different promises that He has made to you, both now and in the future. Every day that you do this, God will increase your knowledge and wisdom, and you will draw closer to Him.

Don't think you can do it? Just think about how much time you spend on one action each day: looking at your screens. So many of us are addicted to our devices. If I am not looking at my laptop, I'm looking at my phone. If I'm not looking at my phone, I'm watching the television. Back to the computer to check my email. Over to the phone to see what's happening on Instagram. Scroll, scroll, scroll some more. It's an endless, addictive cycle that has been purposely designed to function like that by the tech geniuses in Silicon Valley. You can break the cycle by purposely choosing to abide in Him.

Make room for God by cutting back on time spent aimlessly surfing the internet or some social media site, and replace it with time spent in God's presence.

Author C.S. Lewis wrote, "Relying on God has to begin all over again every day as if nothing had yet been done."[11] Every day that we wake up, we need Him. It's probably why Jesus proclaimed in the Lord's Prayer, "Give us this day our daily bread." He didn't say weekly bread or monthly bread; He said *daily bread*.

If you wanted to trade stocks like Warren Buffet, you would read everything about him that you could get your hands on. You would do this daily for years in pursuit of excellence. Then, you would have to put your knowledge into practice. Understanding God's word is far more important. When you do this, you align your attitudes, actions, choices, and other facets of life with the will of God.

A.W. Tozer extolled the need for reading the Bible. He said, "Remember that the Spirit of God inspired the Word and He will be revealed in the Word...if we know the book well enough, we will have an answer to every problem in the world. Every problem that touches you is answered in the Book – stay by the Word. Between those covers is a living Book...God is in the Book. The Holy Spirit is in the Book, and if you want to find Him, go into His Book."[12]

There are several different ways to spend time with God. Daily reading of the Holy Bible teaches His ways and the principles for your life. You can spend time in prayer. You can have conversations with God throughout the day. Each time you perform these activities, you are abiding in Him. Culture has thousands of ways to distract you from conversing with your God, but those ways are only successful if you allow them to be.

Fulton Sheen said, "No soul ever fell away from God without giving up prayer. Prayer is that which establishes contact with Divine Power and opens the invisible resources of heaven. However dark the way, when we pray, temptation can never master us. The first step downward in the average soul is the giving up of the practice of prayer, the breaking of the circuit with the divinity, and the proclamation of one's own self sufficiency." [13]

When you fail to connect with your Maker, you miss out on the benefits He has for you. You are actually cheating yourself, which is tragic but also common. When you reject Christ, you only hurt yourself. I know I have been guilty of this a million times over, but it is never too late to "right the ship," as they say. Abiding in Christ brings with it all sorts of benefits, one of which is the peace that transcends all understanding – peace that overcomes anxiety and worry. Let's abide in the Creator of the universe.

Step Six: Change Your Priorities

> "Put on the full armor of God, so that you can take your stand against the devil's schemes." ~ Ephesians 6:11 (NIV)

Even after you have cast your cares on to the Lord, you will still face attacks from Satan. In preparation for that, you need to put on the full armor of God. Begin by guarding your hearts and minds. Be careful what you intake. If you are watching movies that are loaded with profanities and immoral topics, ask yourself how in the world is that going to draw you closer to the Lord? Every time you intake negative content, you lower the guard on your heart and mind.

When you watch doom-and-gloom news night after night, you grow increasingly pessimistic about the world – and people – around you. Needless to say, this is an issue on both sides of the political aisle.

Imagine what the world would be like if every Christian spent as much time memorizing the word of God for every minute that they watched garbage on their TV or mobile device. Turn off that Mature-rated Netflix show that not only fails to add value to your life but actually strips away a layer of your moral fiber.

I wish I could take back all of the hours I have spent watching absolute trash. The lure of the shows can be overwhelming. Are you mature enough to make the right decision by avoiding negative content and, instead, act productively? There is enough good content out there on the streaming services. You just have to search for it.

Within numerous sections of the Bible, the advice is to focus on God – to fix your eyes on Him. St. Paul advises you to think about what is *true, noble, right, pure, lovely, admirable, excellent,* or *praiseworthy*.[14] With a little thought and planning, you can replace the negative activities in your life with worthy matters.

When you throw off the shackles that hinder you, and you choose to abide in Christ, your confidence grows. You learn with increasing conviction that God cares about every detail of your life. Problems will arise, and when they do, you approach them with more confidence than in times past.

Step Seven: Be Intentional and Practice Daily

How do you know if you have truly cast your cares upon the Lord? If you feel a release of the burden, then you have faithfully thrown your worries and concerns to God. However, if you still feel anxiousness, sadness or worry after committing something to God, then you have not fully cast your cares. You need to revert back to steps three and four, trust in Him and be thankful that He is handling matters for you.

In Philippians 4:6 you are told "Do not be anxious about anything." That's very specific. Do not be anxious, but rather present your needs and be thankful. Only He can see what is truly going on, and only He can solve the problem.

Learning to cast your cares on God can be a struggle at first, but it is a pathway to a God-fearing and eternal mindset. When you fail to cast your cares, you waste time worrying and feeling anxious.

Every time that you cast your cares onto the Lord and He relieves you of the burden, your casting ability is strengthened. Like an athlete who faithfully practices and improves at a skillset, it gets easier for you every time you turn to God with your problems. Your faith increases. Your trust grows. Your confidence grows.

One way to do this is to be intentional. Once a struggle or crisis arises, your first deliberate action should be taking the problem to God. Every trial, however minor, is an opportunity to look beyond your circumstances and to practice casting. The issue may even seem trivial, but it doesn't matter. Everything should be brought to Him, and the small matters of life are the perfect practice grounds.

How often in your life have you had a problem without it even occurring to you to bring it to the Lord first? I wish I had a dollar for every time that situation has occurred in my life. Then, my savings might just rival Bill Gates' fortune. Alright, maybe not, but it's a nice thought!

Reaching out to God right away with your difficulties needs to be a habit. Just like bad habits can become everyday actions without much thought, good habits can work in the same way – but to your benefit.

A fisherman with a long cast sends his line into the deepest of waters where success is most likely. This fisherman developed this skill after years of practice; you need to utilize the same discipline and persistence.

By first bringing your cares and concerns to the Lord, you avoid getting tangled in lines of worry or anxiety. You won't have time for any of that if you immediately cast your cares to Him. When you focus on Him and His word, you drive away doubt, fear and anxiety.

Start today and immediately bring any issues to God's attention. As problems crop up in the days ahead, this instant casting of your cares to God will become a habit.

Chapter Summary

Seven Action Steps to Casting Your Cares to the Lord

Step One: Acknowledge Jesus Christ as Lord and Savior of your life

Step Two: Recognize exactly what your troubles are

Step Three: Believe in Him and trust that He will honor His promises

Step Four: Be thankful that the Lord is relieving you of your burden

Step Five: Learn to abide in Him

Step Six: Set your priorities and eliminate intake that is not beneficial to your life

Step Seven: Practice, practice, and practice again. Practice casting every day

Chapter Six
Biblical Guidance for Casting Our Cares to God

"To the elders among you, I appeal as a fellow elder and a witness of Christ's sufferings who also will share in the glory to be revealed: Be shepherds of God's flock that is under your care, watching over them-not because you must, but because you are willing, as God wants you to be; not pursuing dishonest gain, but eager to serve; not lording it over those entrusted to you, but being examples to the flock. And when the Chief Shepherd appears, you will receive the crown of glory that will never fade away. In the same way, you who are younger, submit yourselves to your elders. All of you, clothe yourselves with humility toward one another, because, 'God opposes the proud but shows favor to the humble.' Humble yourselves, therefore, under God's mighty hand, that he may lift you up in due time. **Cast all your anxiety on him because he cares for you.***"* ~ 1 Peter 5: 1-7 (NIV)

So many times, you see popular verses that are posted online, referenced in books, quoted by pastors, and so on. However, many times you fail to look at the context and the preceding verses. What was God saying right before the well-known verse? That is the question you should always ask because it can help you understand the full story and context of the popular verse. One of the perfect examples of a popular verse is John 3:16: "For God so loved the world that he gave his one and only Son, that whoever believes in him shall not perish but have eternal life."[1] When Tim Tebow had "John 3:16" painted under his eyes prior to televised football games, including the National Championship game, online searches for this verse went through the roof. In fact, 94 million people searched online for that exact Bible verse.[2]

Another example of a popular verse is Philippians 4:13, in which St. Paul said, "I can do all things through Christ which strengthens me."[3] In the verses prior to 4:13, Paul discusses why he has learned to be content in all circumstances. He pleads with us to focus on things that are honest, pure and true. It's really a fascinating chapter, but I wonder how many people who are familiar with this one verse know that Paul wrote it from jail? Context is vital, and reading the entire scripture is important to the Christian seeking to apply the principles.

The famous verse, 1 Peter 5:7, is no exception: "Cast all your anxiety on Him because He cares for you." In this Apostolic letter, Peter begins by addressing the elders of the church and instructs them to be shepherds of the flock they are in charge over, and to do so willingly. He says, "Be shepherds of God's flock that is under your care, watching over them—not because you must, but because you are willing..."⁴ Then, Peter specifically says not to pursue "dishonest gain, but [be] eager to serve; not lording it over those entrusted to you, but being examples to the flock."⁵

Peter then switches audiences and tells the congregation to submit themselves to the elders: "In the same way, you who are younger, submit yourselves to your elders." This instruction all works together, because if the elders follow Peter's advice and set the proper example, then the congregation follows suit.

Peter continues to tell the entire audience to be humble, submit themselves to the Lord, and avoid pride: "All of you, clothe yourselves with humility toward one another, because, 'God opposes the proud but shows favor to the humble.' **Humble yourselves, therefore, under God's mighty hand, that he may lift you up in due time.**"⁶

Those are the requirements given to the Christians prior to the famous verse, 1 Peter 5:7: "Cast all your anxiety on Him because He cares for you."

Are you just to avoid the prior verses and focus on the ones you want? Of course not. When you received instruction in school, the teacher did not just pick and choose a few lines from the lesson book and focus only on those. The entire textbook was used in your education, because it all worked together.

You learn the foundation to casting your cares on to the Lord in the beginning of 1 Peter 5. Right before the verse about casting your cares to the Lord, he gives some specific instructions. Submit to the elders. Be caretakers of the flock (the church community). Avoid pride. Be humble.

> "If you should ask me what are the ways of God, I would tell you that the first is humility, the second is humility, and the third is humility. Not that there are no other precepts to give, but if humility does not precede all that you do, your efforts are fruitless."[7] ~ St. Augustine of Hippo

In Psalm 86, David petitions the Lord, "Hear me, Lord, and answer me, for I am poor and needy."[8]

First be humble, then cast all your anxiety on Him because He cares for you.

An entire book could be written about humility. Culture today "rewards" those who are the opposite of humble. Post your amazing life on social media and rack up as many likes as possible. The more comments, the more "love" tags, and the more "shares," the more popular you apparently are. This results in a happy, fulfilling life, right? No, of course not. In fact, social media use has been linked to increased levels of depression and suicide.[9]

Humility is an obligation for Christians. It is not a choice but a virtue that you are directed to obtain and live out in your lives. It is anti-cultural, which makes it all the more difficult to do. It also proves your faith when you successfully humble your lives to the Lord.

If you follow the process provided to you in 1 Peter, then it is very unlikely that you would ruminate about your problems. When you have followed God's advice, and you have thrown your cares into the Lord's lap, those issues become His to deal with now. You just sit back, continue to pray, be thankful for the outcome, continue to heed His advice, and wait for the results.

If you continue to worry about whatever it is that is bothering you, then you are not trusting in God and you are not trusting in His word. Throw it to him. Cast and let go.

What good has ever come of worry? Instead of making you stronger, worry weakens you. Instead of doing God's will, when you worry, you rely on your own meager strength and willpower.

Remember Philippians 4:8: "Finally, brothers and sisters, whatever is true, whatever is noble, whatever is right, whatever is pure, whatever is lovely, whatever is admirable—if anything is excellent or praiseworthy—think about such things."[10] When you worry, you focus on the negative or the possible bad scenario that could happen instead of dwelling on the items commanded to you in Philippians 4:8.

Action Item

Replace your negative thoughts and habits with a mindset that dwells on what is true, noble, right, pure, lovely, admirable, excellent, or praiseworthy.

Overheard in an Orchard

Said the Robin to the Sparrow:
"I should really like to know
Why these anxious human beings
Rush about and worry so."

Said the Sparrow to the Robin:
"Friend, I think that it must be
That they have no heavenly Father
Such as cares for you and me."
– *Elizabeth Cheney*

Chapter Seven

Experience is the Teacher

"I will turn all my mountains into roads, and my highways will be raised up." ~ Isaiah 49:11 (NIV)

My mother-in-law Patty wanted to go to Yellowstone National Park. I really had no interest. It wasn't the type of trip that was on the top of my vacation getaways. Reluctantly, in the winter of 2019, I began to research everything involved in traveling from Florida and going out west. We had good friends who had traveled to Yellowstone the year before, and their insight was invaluable. They gave us several flyers and maps that they had saved.

Despite our friends' help and all of the information that I could dig up online, I quickly realized one thing – this trip was a big undertaking. Given the enormity of the area, it was very difficult for someone who had never been there to understand where one should really stay. Just deciding where to stay was a difficult and very important decision. Choose poorly, and it could affect the entire trip. The area was so large and spread out that if I chose our lodging in the wrong location, we could be looking at an hour to two-hour drive just to reach the popular spots within the park.

My wife and I overlooking the phenomenal Grand Prismatic in Yellowstone National Park

Finally, after many, many hours of research and deliberation, I ended up booking a total of four hotels. We would start in Idaho, then West Yellowstone, on to a town south of Jackson and finally back to a hotel near the airport in Salt Lake City. It was a lot of driving, but in the end, it was worth it. Yellowstone Park, Jackson Hole, and the Grant Tetons were spectacular.

Having never been there and having never experienced Big Sky country, it was impossible to really know what it would be like until we actually got there.

Life is like that. You can be "book smart," but if you haven't already experienced what you learned about in the classroom, you really do not know the intricacies of the topic. You don't know the area because you have never been there.

Personal Experience – Put to the Test

While working on this book, I prayed to the Lord for stories. I wanted to be able to convey to the readers stories that best illustrate casting your cares to God. Most readers love stories because they can relate to them. People love hearing captivating stories in which others have overcome struggles and proven victorious in the end. It is one of the big reasons why movies like *Rudy, The Shawshank Redemption, Rocky,* and many others are so endearing to millions of people.

Of course, it came with little surprise that the Lord had to give our family a first-hand example.

In early April of 2021, our middle daughter Genesis, age seven, was complaining about going to the potty. What we saw in the toilet shocked my wife and I. There is no way to sugar coat it. It was a bloody, mess – extremely gross diarrhea. To our dismay, her bowel movements failed to improve over the course of the next few days. My wife took her to the pediatrician who ran some blood tests.

Genesis was put on a BRAT diet, a bland mix of foods consisting of bananas, rice, and other unappealing fare. One or two days of this wasn't too bad, but it would last significantly longer than that. The following week, the test results came back negative. However, Genesis failed to improve. In the meantime, she was losing both weight and blood.

Early the following week, we took her to a pediatric gastroenterologist and hematologist. She ran additional tests and told us to continue to keep our daughter on a limited diet.

It was now early May and the weekend consisted of the final days for the Florida State Fair. Our kids, having not been in years, wanted to go. We took the three of them on Sunday, the final day. Genesis did fine, but at times throughout the day she was extremely irritable. As a parent this was a little annoying considering that we were spending a hot, expensive day at the fair.

That evening after we returned home, Genesis had probably the most horrific bowel movement I had witnessed over the past several weeks. In addition, I noticed how much weight she had lost. The following morning, I came out of my bedroom and found her sitting on the floor outside my door. She was in a weak and frail state. I told my wife that we had to take her to the ER if we didn't get answers from the doctor.

We did get her into the doctor that afternoon. The additional tests had proven negative, so the next step was going to be a colonoscopy to determine what was really going on with her intestines.

On Tuesday, May 4, 2021, I took off from work and drove Genesis to St. Joseph Children's Hospital in Tampa. Admitting your child into the hospital is no easy task, and it is very hard to relate to if you haven't experienced it as a parent.

It is truly heartbreaking to think of all the parents who spend weeks, months, or in the worst cases, much longer timeframes with their children at the hospital.

My wife and I took turns and spent most of the week with Genesis in the hospital. Needless to say, it didn't take long for things to get old, especially for our usually vibrant seven-year-old daughter.

On day three we got the results back from the colonoscopy that our girl had what we suspected – Ulcerative Colitis. This is a chronic gastro issue that has no cure and is a condition that has to be managed for the rest of the patient's life. It was not what we wanted to hear, but we also knew that the diagnosis could have been much worse.

Over the course of the next several weeks, we learned to adjust as a family to the new normal of Genesis' diet, medication, and restrictions. Her siblings had to learn quickly to be considerate of the fact that they could still eat pretty much anything they wanted -- within reason, of course, and with Mom and Dad's permission – while Genesis had to do without some of her favorite foods.

My wife and I had to learn how to respond to our daughter's tantrums as they related to her diet. Genesis was on the steroid Prednisone in the beginning, and if anyone looked at her the wrong way, she would rip their head off – figuratively speaking, of course. A hungry seven-year-old girl on a corticosteroid is no laughing matter.

Genesis had to learn to trust God and trust Mom and Dad more than she had in the past. It was going to be OK, but life would be a little different from here on out.

From the beginning of this process, I had to learn to put my lessons here into action. It's always easier instructing others on how they should behave in a crisis, but when it comes to your own situation, the solution can often seem much harder to implement.

When Genesis first got ill, I was very worried. When I found her sitting outside my bedroom that morning, looking very ill and lethargic, it was scary. I had to cast my cares to the Lord and put the situation in His hands.

Over the next several weeks, as we simply had no idea what the future held, we would be put to the test. Our entire family had to fling our worries and anxieties about Genesis' situation to the Lord, confident that He would hold her in His hands and bring healing to her body.

And He did just that. The diagnosis was a big adjustment to our family and a huge adjustment to the life that Genesis had known in her prior 7 ½ years, but we got through the early months about as well as could be expected. Ulcerative Colitis is a life-long condition, so I am sure we will have our ups and downs over the next few years, but God's got this.

On a lighter note, in December of 2022, I took my family to see the King And Country's Little Drummer Boy concert. I had five mobile tickets to Amalie Arena in Tampa, Florida for the Friday night showing on December 9, or so I thought. After fighting horrible Friday night traffic heading into Tampa, we arrived, along with a large crowd, at the arena where the Tampa Bay Lightning play. We navigated our way through the heavy security line, got the green light, and headed to another line to show our tickets to the bar code scanner. That's when our problems started. My mobile tickets would not work, and we were not allowed to enter.

Leaving the family behind, I headed back the way I came, down the stairs outside the arena to the Ticket Office on the first floor.

Finally, the problem was discovered. I had purchased five tickets to Amway Center in Orlando, Florida for Saturday night. Going to that was not an option for me, so I purchased five new tickets to the show we were trying to get into. Worse seats in the upper deck at a similar price to my seats in 109.

I was not happy. In the past this would have ruined my night, but I was determined to not let that happen. We were going to enjoy the show, 'like it or not!' Cast your cares to the Lord, right?

As usual, the show was great. We headed home after a late night and put the kids to bed. I quickly posted the tickets for sale online, knowing that getting help from TicketMaster was unlikely. There was a small window of opportunity to sell the Orlando tickets, and I was not very hopeful I could get my money back.

I sold two of the tickets by late morning on Saturday. While attending the local Christmas parade, I was learning how to transfer the tickets via the TicketMaster app. I was also searching all over the app trying to get a hold of someone at the company to explain my dilemma, hoping that a sympathetic ear would lead to an easy refund for the three remaining tickets. I finally got a hold of someone via the chat (which was near impossible to find) and was told that the only thing that could be done was an exchange...for the same event! Thanks for nothing.

Around 2 pm, just hours before show time, I received another text from an interested buyer. They were interested in possibly all three tickets. I convinced them that I was not a scammer, and I was able to unload the remainder of the concert tickets. Happy to get my money back, I transferred the tickets online.

This nice couple from the Orlando area explained to me that they were watching holiday movies on Friday night and the wife, on a whim, just happened to check if one of her favorite bands for King And Country were ever coming to their area. They were, the next night!

A Boy Named Abraham

The following morning, I was greeted by an ecstatic text from the couple that purchased the remaining three tickets.

"This concert is insane," began the conversation. "My wife is from Mexico and we sponsored a five-year-old boy named Abraham!"

At their concerts Joel and Luke Smallbone of for King And Country tell the story of how their large family immigrated from Australia with little money on the promise of a job for their Dad. Unfortunately, he soon lost that job and the Smallbone family was left destitute. As a struggling family they were helped out in so many ways, sometimes by people they didn't even know. Today, the talented artists spend part of every concert trying to gain sponsors for Compassion International, a non-profit that does amazing work in developing countries.

As I get older, I find that I make more mistakes in areas where I would not have in the past. One of these mistakes was purchasing five concert events for an event in the wrong city. It could have ruined my night, but it didn't. It led to a boy named Abraham who now has a sponsored from a family in America. Through Compassion International, Abraham can now attend classes, overcome illiteracy, learn about Jesus, and gain many benefits for his entire family.

What seemed like a very costly and frustrating mistake at the time led to a great ending. Casting your cares to God is always the right decision.

Chapter Eight
Control Your Intake

It will be much easier to cast your cares to God, if you can abide in Him. Make room for Him by discriminating and curating what you allow into your life.

In Ephesians 4:29, St. Paul writes, "Do not let any unwholesome talk come out of your mouths, but only what is helpful for building others up according to their needs, that it may benefit those who listen."[1]

Proverbs 12:25 says, "Anxiety in a man's heart weighs it down, but a good word cheers it up."[2]

From the very first line in the Book of John, God describes Himself as "The Word."

Words are powerful. You have the choice to use your words to edify one another and yourself. Thousands of books have been written on self-talk, and there is a good reason for that. It is human nature to struggle with self-talk.

Self-talk comes in many different ways. You may constantly remind yourself that you "are not any good" at such and such, or that you "always screw up."

Other negative self-talk could be "what ifs." What if my spouse stops loving me? What if my kids get into drugs? What if my car breaks down and I can't pay to get it fixed? The 'what if' scenarios are infinite.

Jesus warns you about the "what ifs of life" in Matthew 6:25-34: "Therefore I tell you, do not worry about your life, what you will eat or drink; or about your body, what you will wear. Is not life more than food, and the body more than clothes? Look at the birds of the air; they do not sow or reap or store away in barns, and yet your heavenly Father feeds them. Are you not much more valuable than they? Can any one of you by worrying add a single hour to your life?"

"And why do you worry about clothes? See how the flowers of the field grow. They do not labor or spin. Yet I tell you that not even Solomon in all his splendor was dressed like one of these. If that is how God clothes the grass of the field, which is here today and tomorrow is thrown into the fire, will he not much more clothe you—you of little faith? So do not worry, saying, 'What shall we eat?' or 'What shall we drink?' or 'What shall we wear?' For the pagans run after all these things, and your heavenly Father knows that you need them. But seek first his kingdom and his righteousness, and all these things will be given to you as well. Therefore do not worry about tomorrow, for tomorrow will worry about itself. Each day has enough trouble of its own."

Just as important as your self-talk is the talk that you hear throughout the day. Do you have a friend who is constantly spewing negative words or ugly tales? Are you watching news channels that are getting you stirred up? Are you viewing movies or shows where profanity is littered throughout the story?

All of these intakes can impact your current state of mind and your overall mental well-being.

If you are constantly bombarded with bad news and negativity, it is unlikely that you will be going about your day with joy in your heart and a hop in your step. You have to be careful what you are intaking, and this can come from friends you hang around, websites you visit, news shows you watch, and more.

In order to cast your cares to God, you need to control your intake and abide in Him. Time is a precious commodity that you never get back. What can you do instead of watching your favorite news channel or scrolling endlessly down your favorite website?

Action Items

Figure out two sources of negative intakes and eliminate them from your schedule this week.

Replace the time you save with time that you can abide in God.

Chapter Nine
The Freedom of the Son

The parable of the prodigal son is probably the most well known parable in the Bible, and many of you have heard it numerous times. I can't tell you how many times I've heard this parable preached on in my life, but safe to say, it's been a bunch.

As the story[1] goes in Luke Chapter 15:

"There was a man who had two sons. And the younger of them said to his father, 'Father, give me the share of property that is coming to me.' And he divided his property between them. Not many days later, the younger son gathered all he had and took a journey into a far country, and there he squandered his property in reckless living. And when he had spent everything, a severe famine arose in that country, and he began to be in need. So, he went and hired himself out to one of the citizens of that country, who sent him into his fields to feed pigs. And he was longing to be fed with the pods that the pigs ate, and no one gave him anything.

"But when he came to himself, he said, 'How many of my father's hired servants have more than enough bread, but I perish here with hunger! I will arise and go to my father, and I will say to him, "Father, I have sinned against heaven and before you. I am no longer worthy to be called your son. Treat me as one of your hired servants."' And he arose and came to his father. But while he was still a long way off, his father saw him and felt compassion, and ran and embraced him and kissed him. And the son said to him, 'Father, I have sinned against heaven and before you. I am no longer worthy to be called your son.' But the father said to his servants, 'Bring quickly the best robe, and put it on him, and put a ring on his hand, and shoes on his feet. And bring the fattened calf and kill it, and let us eat and celebrate. For this my son was dead, and is alive again; he was lost, and is found.' And they began to celebrate.

"Now his older son was in the field, and as he came and drew near to the house, he heard music and dancing. And he called one of the servants and asked what these things meant. And he said to him, 'Your brother has come, and your father has killed the fattened calf, because he has received him back safe and sound.' But he was angry and refused to go in. His father came out and entreated him, but he answered his father, 'Look, these many years I have served you, and I never disobeyed your command, yet you never gave me a young goat, that I might celebrate with my friends. But when this son of yours came, who has devoured your property with prostitutes, you killed the fattened calf for him!' And he said to him, 'Son, you are always with me, and all that is mine is yours.

It was fitting to celebrate and be glad, for this your brother was dead, and is alive; he was lost, and is found.'"

There are a lot of angles to this story, including one that has probably hit many people hard – the jealous brother. He is easy to relate to, because who hasn't acted or felt that way?

However, there was one aspect of this parable that I just never really thought deeply about. To me the story was always about the son wanting to cash in on his inheritance and go have fun. But it was a lot more than that. It was about freedom for the son. He could finally leave home, be his own boss, and do whatever he wanted. Life was good! He had ditched the old man and his stupid brother, and he was free to make his own decisions.

Rembrandt's Painting 'The Return of the Prodigal Son'

This is exactly how life is. God gives you the free will to make your own choices. We are all like the prodigal son who had the opportunity to use his time, money, and resources in whatever way he wanted. Unfortunately for the son, he chose poorly, and his bad decisions quickly led to dire consequences.

Hitting rock bottom, the prodigal son was forced to take a job where he spent the whole day feeding pigs. The animals had a better life than he did. The son finally made a wise decision and decided that he must return to his father and seek forgiveness.

While the son was still a far way off...

This is one of the best and most revealing lines in the Holy Bible. "But while he was still a long way off, his father saw him and felt compassion, and ran and embraced him and kissed him." The son didn't even have to make it all the way back to the father. The father ran to him and loved him.

In life you are free to make your own decisions, but oftentimes you have to pay the consequences for those choices.

The great news is that you do not have to be perfect and have a sinless life before you can cast your whole self to the Lord. It is indeed a very good thing, because being perfect is not a possibility for any of us.

While you are "still a long way off," if you turn back to Him, the Father will run to you and save you. How amazing is that?

The key is to cast your pride, your sin, and all of your bad decisions to the Lord.

> "Humble yourself before the Lord and He will lift you up." ~ James 4:10 (NIV)

Like the prodigal son you must admit that you have sinned against God and that you are helpless without Him. In turn, the Father doesn't just forgive you and accept you, he runs to you.

Action Item

Identify one area in your life where you are disobeying your Father in heaven. Cast this sin to Him and ask for forgiveness. Leave this sin with Him, admitting that you can not fix it on your own strength.

Chapter Ten
Some of Our Cares?

In 1 Peter 5:7, you are instructed to give your cares to the Lord. Cast to God some of your financial problems. Throw him some of your relationship issues but certainly not the ones that you can take care of yourself. Give him the problems you are having with your children, but the ones with your siblings or spouse, you will take care of those.

Work issues? You can deal with that. Besides, you understand what the problem is; you just have to figure out the solution that will work.

Concerned about your culture and where the country is heading? Maybe you will cast those cares to God because, surely, He can help with those issues.

Some things you will take care of, and some things you will let God handle. It's your decision based on your infinite wisdom and experience.

Sound ridiculous? It is. In 1 Peter 5:7, you are instructed to cast ALL of your cares to the Lord. Not some. Not a few. Not the ones you pick and choose. Anything that you are concerned about should be cast to Him. Is anything exempt from His concern? No, not according to scripture. There is nothing exempt from the instruction not to worry about anything, but rather, pray about everything.

It is why the word "all" is used in the verse. Scripture does not say "some" or a "few" or "select." It says "all." Cast all of your cares.

A complimentary verse is found in Proverbs 3:5-6. "Trust in the Lord with all your heart and lean not on your own understanding, but in all your ways acknowledge the Lord, and He will make your paths straight."[1]

There's that word "all" again.

Like most of God's instructions, it's easier said than done.

The only way to cast all of your cares to Him is to make it a habit. Like any habit, the more often you do it, the more it becomes grooved into the recesses of your brain. Practice, practice, and yes, practice some more.

Every time that you bring your cares to Him, even the most mundane, you are learning to trust and rely on His goodness.

You can take baby steps. The next time something is troubling you, throw it into the Lord's lap. Since for most of you, not a day goes by without some type of trouble, it is easy to get started!

Start today.

Someone cuts you off in traffic. Someone is rude to you at a store. Instead of reacting as you might have in the past, cast your cares.

"God, I give You my frustration."

"Lord, I give You my anger. Help that big jerk make better decisions and to know You!"

"Jesus, take over this thought for me. I need Your help and I appreciate You handling this problem for me."

> **"Be strong in the Lord and in his mighty power.** Put on the full armor of God, so that you can take your stand against the devil's schemes." ~Ephesians 6:10-11 (NIV)

In his letter to the church at Ephesus in Asia Minor, Paul provides specific instructions to battle your spiritual demons. He does not say, "Be strong in your mighty power." You should know from experience, as Paul did, that that is a fruitless exercise. Only God and His mighty power can handle what you throw at Him. Only God and His mighty power can stand against the devil's schemes. Satan has a lot of schemes, and one of them is to convince you that you can handle your own problems without God's help.

Every time that you are given some type of trouble, you are also given the opportunity to cast your cares onto the Lord. It is an opportunity to surrender your control to Him and trust that He will do what He says He will do.

Every time that He gives you peace in these situations, a good habit of trusting in Him and casting your cares to Him is re-enforced. Practice makes perfect.

Action Item

This week deliberately find some everyday situations where you can choose to cast your cares to God.

Run To The Father by Matt Maher

I've carried a burden
For too long on my own
I wasn't created
To bear it alone
I hear Your invitation
To let it all go
I see it now
I'm laying it down
I know that I need You
I run to the Father
Fall into grace
I'm done with the hiding
No reason to wait
My heart needs a surgeon
My soul needs a friend
So I'll run to the Father
Again and again
And again and again...

Source: Musixmatch
Songwriters: Matt Maher / Ran Jackson / Cody Carnes
Run To The Father lyrics © Be Essential Songs

Chapter Eleven
His Eyes Are on the Sparrow

"Look at the birds of the air; they neither sow nor reap nor gather into barns, and yet your heavenly Father feeds them. Are you not of more value than they?"
~ Matthew 6:26 (ESV)

Mrs. Martin explained that early in the spring of 1905, her and her husband were sojourning in Elmira, New York.

"We contracted a deep friendship for a couple by the name of Mr. and Mrs. Doolittle—true saints of God. Mrs. Doolittle had been bedridden for nigh twenty years. Her husband was an incurable cripple who had to propel himself to and from his business in a wheelchair. Despite their afflictions, they lived happy Christian lives, bringing inspiration and comfort to all who knew them. One day while we were visiting with the Doolittles, my husband commented on their bright hopefulness and asked them for the secret of it. Mrs. Doolittle's response was simple: 'His eye is on the sparrow, and I know He watches me.' [1]

This meeting would lead Civilla Durfee Martin, a schoolteacher with modest musical training, to write one of the most influential gospel hymns of all time. "His Eye is on the Sparrow" has been performed by the likes of Gladys Knight, Whitney Houston, Marvin Gaye, Kirk Franklin, and Barbara Mandrell.

> "Are not two sparrows sold for a farthing? And one of them shall not fall on the ground without your Father's care. But the very hairs of your head are all numbered. Fear ye not therefore, ye are of more value than many sparrows." ~ Matthew 10: 29-31(KJB)

Why should you feel discouraged? When His eye is on the sparrow and He values you way more than a small bird.

Why should the shadows come? Why should your heart be lonely? His eye is on the sparrow and you are worth far more than the sparrow. In fact, you are worth far more than many sparrows.

You can take great comfort in the verses found in chapters 6 and 10 of Matthew's Gospel, because God clearly tells you how much He values you.

Even the hairs on your head are numbered. How detailed is that? If God cares enough to number your hairs, wouldn't it make sense that He cares that much more about the very smallest of details in your life?

When you realize that the Lord is actually concerned about your small details, that changes your perspective. God is not some absentee father. He is ready and willing to hear about all of your problems.

He watches over each and every one of his children.

The disciple Nathaniel meets Jesus for the first time, according to John 1:48, and he immediately questions the Messiah, "How do you know me?" Jesus stuns Nathaniel with his answer: "Before Phillip called you, when you were under the fig tree, I saw you." Nathaniel knew instantly that this was the son of God.

Nathaniel was all alone underneath the fig tree. He was alone with his thoughts and innermost desires. How could Jesus have seen him under the fig tree?

His eye is on the sparrow. His eye is on you and me, every day at every moment. In every situation His eye is on you.

When you take that perspective, it becomes easier to cast your cares on to Him.

Action Item

Sit still and contemplate that God cares about the smallest of details.

Chapter Twelve
A Treasure Trove of Blessings

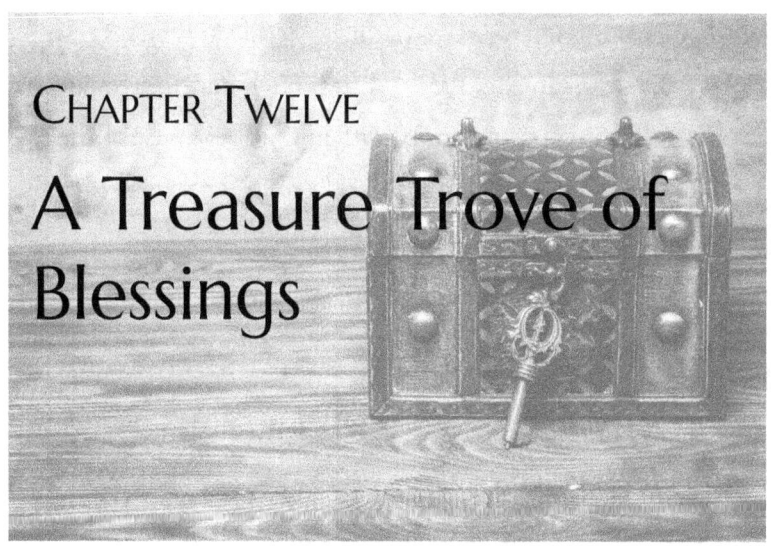

One of the last times I delt with depression and anxiety, I was led to create a gratitude journal. I began to fill this book of blank pages with all the many blessings in my life. I would also document the times that the Lord came through for me and lifted me out of whatever difficult situation I was in. With this journal close at hand on my nightstand, having these easily-accessible reminders was invaluable in times when I needed to remember how good the Lord is.

Mother Mary "pondered these things in her heart" when Jesus was born and during His childhood. Is there any doubt that she would have relied on these wonderful memories when Jesus was unjustly imprisoned, brought to trial, tortured and then nailed to a cross? Mary didn't have a journal at her access, but the mother of God kept the memories stored in her heart.

This is just one of many reasons to keep a gratitude journal. Every time God is faithful, you can record those great memories in your journal and refer back to them, especially in times of distress. When you are troubled, so often your thoughts are fixated on what is currently going on. It can be difficult, in the midst of the fire, to recall all of the times God came through for you in your life. Having a gratitude journal changes all that.

David's Confidence

Like Mary, another famous character in the Bible used the same strength of gratitude to fight his battles. The first book of Samuel, tells the famous tale of David and Goliath. The monster-sized Philistine has been tormenting the Israelites morning and nights for 40 days. No one is willing to face the giant for fear of death and humiliation. If anyone dared to take on Goliath and lost, the Israelites would become the subjects of the Philistines. Not one person in the entire army had the faith and courage to fight Goliath.

However, David had a history of success with the Lord. As a shepherd, young David had taken on the most vicious of wild animals to save his sheep. It is with that confidence that he approaches King Saul and asks for permission to fight Goliath. Eyeing David and determining that he had no chance against the adversary, Saul initially rejects the request. David responds by recounting his past successes.

"Your servant used to tend his father's sheep, and whenever a lion or bear came to carry off a sheep from the flock, I would go after it and attack it and rescue the prey from its mouth. If it attacked me, I would seize it by the jaw, strike it, and kill it. Your servant has killed both a lion and a bear, and this uncircumcised Philistine will be as one of them, because he has insulted the armies of the living God.

The Lord, who delivered me from the claws of the lion and the bear, will also keep me safe from the clutches of this Philistine."

Saul is sold. "Go!" exclaims the King. "The Lord will be with you."

Most of you know the rest of the story. David bravely approaches the giant, who mocks the young shepherd.

"You come against me with sword and spear and scimitar, but I come against you in the name of the Lord of hosts, the God of the armies of Israel that you have insulted. Today the Lord shall deliver you into my hand," proclaims David. After grimly describing how he will kill him, David continues, "Thus, the whole land shall learn [this day] that Israel has a God. All this multitude, too, shall learn it is not by sword or spear that the Lord saves. For the battle is the Lord's, and He shall deliver you into our hands." [1]

With just one of his stones, David strikes the Philistine down and delivers victory into the hands of the stunned soldiers of Israel.

Taking on what seems to be an impossible task, David is briming with confidence because he remembers all of the times that the Lord has come through for him. Your story may not be as dramatic and historic as David's, but you can do the same.

It is vital to document all of the blessings in your life and all of the times that God has kept His promise so that you will have at your fingertips ammunition to fight the spiritual battle when it comes your way. And it will come your way.

Satan is coming hard at you because he knows what you can accomplish when you rely on the Lord. No one is immune.

By keeping a record of your victories, you can never forget all of the blessing you have and all of the times that the Lord has fought for you and your family.

Action Item

Start a gratitude journal today and begin to document all your many blessings and all the times God has taken care of you.

Add to the journal every time a prayer is answered and every time God has watched over you and your family.

Chapter Thirteen

Real World Examples

"Because God has made you for himself, our hearts are restless until we rest in him." ~ St. Augustine of Hippo

Hope Darst was on the music worship team at The Belonging church in Nashville, Tennessee. This was a church founded just a few years ago, in 2014, by Henry and Alex Seeley in the basement of their home.

Early in her journey at The Belonging, Hope was asked to be a part of the music writing team for the church. While away at a conference retreat, she got together with friends Mia Fieldes and Andrew Holt, both of whom were on the worship team.

Mia shared with her friends that she was in a season of battling a lot of fear and anxiety. Hope's friend expressed the disappointment that God's promise in her life was falling apart at this time. Mia's vulnerability opened the door for Hope to express her intense struggles with insecurity, stress, and anxiety.

The result was something amazing.

Peace Be Still

"Something began to happen in that room," explained Hope. "You could feel the presence of God."

"So, we did the only thing we knew to do that day; we declared peace over ourselves," continued Hope. "We knew that if we could sing God's promises over ourselves, it would drown out the fear and would shift things inside of us.

"Fear and anxiety don't just disappear because we write songs or sing songs, but God has given us a weapon of worship to use every time the wave of fear wants to raise itself against us. This song is a prayer and a weapon; a prayer of peace over everything you are facing and a weapon of worship to defeat fear, depression, and doubt. God has promised us peace."

Hope explained that it was Mia who first said, "I don't want to be afraid." That turned into "I don't want to be afraid every time I face the waves."[1]

As of this writing, the music videos for "Peace Be Still" have over three million views, and the song has changed thousands of lives.

Peace Be Still Lyrics[2]

I don't want to be afraid
Every time I face the waves
I don't want to be afraid
I don't want to be afraid
I don't want to fear the storm
Just because I hear it roar
I don't want to fear the storm
I don't want to fear the storm
Peace be still
Say the word and I will
Set my feet upon the sea
Till I'm dancing in the deep
Peace be still
You are here so it is well
Even when my eyes can't see
I will trust the voice that speaks
I'm not gonna be afraid
'Cause these waves are only waves
I'm not gonna be afraid
No I'm not gonna be afraid
And I'm not gonna fear the storm
You are greater than it's roar
Oh I'm not gonna fear the storm
No I'm not gonna fear at all
Peace be still...

For Such A Time As This

Kayleigh McEnany rose from a small town in Dade City, Florida, to attend both Brown and Oxford Universities. Her amazing path eventually led her to a role in the White House under the 45th president of the United States, Donald J. Trump. In the spring of 2020, Kayleigh became the 33rd White House Press Secretary, a job that would put her right in the firing line of a press that was chomping at the bit to disparage the President at every conceivable opportunity. To say that this was a stressful and high-pressure job would be the understatement of the year. However, Kayleigh had been through challenging times before, and she knew how...and who to put her faith in.

Two years prior to reaching this nationally prominent role, Kayleigh was faced with a life-changing decision. Eight members of her family, mostly aunts and cousins on her maternal side, had suffered with breast cancer. The disease hit some of them in their early twenties. Kayleigh's mom had tested positive for the BRCA 2 gene, which gave her approximately an 84% chance of contracting breast cancer. Consequently, she would have a preventative double mastectomy.

Nine years later, Kayleigh decided to have the same test to see if she also was inflicted with the BRCA 2 gene. It was positive.

With the full support of her family, Kayleigh made the same difficult decision as her mother to have a double mastectomy. She cast her cares to the Lord and put her full trust in Him.

"A day prior to the surgery, while flying home to Florida, I gazed out the window and down to earth when the lyrics of "Carry Me Through" played, reminding me that I would be climbing the mountain before me with the strength of Jesus Christ replacing my own.[3]

He carried me through with His strength. He also gave me a peace – that same peace that I found when I went from tears in my West Wing office to total and complete serenity at the podium [in her job as Press Secretary]. Despite my apprehension in the night leading up to the surgery, I had a strange calm in the pre-operation bed before being wheeled back to the surgery."

Two years later on the stage of the Republican National Convention, Kayleigh would bravely recount her story in front of an audience of over 17 million viewers.

When you confidently cast your cares to the Lord and then tell others about it, it pays dividends. "To this day, I still have women come up to me and say how much that speech meant to them," explains Kayleigh in her memoir *For Such a Time as This*. "Some have breast cancer. Some have genetic mutations. Every story is unique. One in eight women will be diagnosed with breast cancer in their lifetime. As women, we fight this together."[4]

It is Well with My Soul

Imagine losing your four-year-old son to scarlet fever in 1871. A few months later a massive fire in Chicago then wipes out numerous properties that you owned, costing you a large part of your fortune. Two years later in 1873, you have a trip planned to Europe for you, your wife, and your four daughters. Important business dealings, involving the rebuild from the fire, prevent you from departing on schedule. You decide to send your family on the mid-November trip with plans to meet them at a later date.

A week later, tragedy strikes again. In the early hours of November 22, 1873, the Ville du Havre carrying 313 passengers and crew collides with a British iron clipper. In only twelve minutes the ship sinks and 226 people on board die. Among them are Horatio Spafford's four daughters. His wife Anna survives and will later telegram her husband, "Saved alone. What shall I do..."

How do you respond? Horatio Spafford immediately departs for England to meet up with the sole survivor of his family. Approaching the spot where the Ville du Havre sank, the captain notified Horatio to inform him that they were passing over the approximate location of the tragedy.

Horatio had an eternal mindset and that mindset allowed him to cast all his cares to the Lord, no matter how great. Here at this grim segment of the voyage, he was inspired to pen the lyrics to what would become one of the most beloved Christian songs of all time.

It Is Well With My Soul

When peace like a river attendeth my way
When sorrows like sea billows roll
Whatever my lot, Thou hast taught me to say
It is well, it is well with my soul
It is well (it is well)
With my soul (with my soul)
It is well, it is well with my soul
Though Satan should buffet, though trials should come
Let this blest assurance control
That Christ (yes, He has) has regarded my helpless estate
And has shed His own blood for my soul
It is well (it is well)
With my soul (with my soul)
It is well, it is well with my soul
My sin, oh the bliss of this glorious thought (a thought)
My sin, not in part, but the whole (every bit, every bit, all of it)
Is nailed to the cross, and I bear it no more (yes)
Praise the Lord, praise the Lord, O my soul
It is well (it is well)
With my soul (with my soul)
It is well, it is well with my soul
Sing it as well
It is well (it is well)
With my soul (with my soul)
It is well, it is well with my soul
And Lord, haste the day when my faith shall be sight

The clouds be rolled back as a scroll
The trump shall resound, and the Lord shall descend
Even so, it is well with my soul
It is well (it is well)
With my soul (with my soul)
It is well, it is well with my soul
'Cause of You, Jesus, it is well
It is well (it is well)
With my soul (with my soul)
It is well, it is well with my soul

Following the sinking of the Ville du Havre, Horatio's wife Anna gave birth to three children. The Spaffords would go on to become missionaries in the holy city of Jerusalem, where they set up a utopian society known as the American Colony. There, they also adopted a fourth child, a boy named Jacob. To add further to the Spafford legacy, Jacob discovered the Siloam Inscription, the only known extant inscription from ancient Israel and Judah which commemorates a public construction work. The Siloam Inscription confirms Biblical accounts of the Monarchic Period[5] and the existence of the Gihon spring and Hezekiah's Tunnel which are referenced multiple times in the Old Testament.[6]

In January, 2023, news broke that the Pool of Siloam, a biblical site cherished by both Christians and Jews and the location where Jesus healed the blind man, was being excavated and would soon be open to the public for the first time in over 2,000 years.

"One of most significant sites affirming Jerusalem's biblical heritage — not simply as a matter of faith, but as a matter of fact — with significance to billions around the world, will be made fully accessible for the first time in 2,000 years," explained Ze'ev Orenstein, director of international affairs for the City of David Foundation in Jerusalem.[7]

Horatio did not give up when he faced an inconceivable tragedy. His legacy stands today as a testament to never losing faith in a loving God.

Imprisoned With ISIS

Remember Petr Jasek? While in the country to help persecuted Christians, this missionary was accosted at the airport by Sudan officials and taken to an interrogation room. What he initially thought was a routine question-and-answer session became something far more serious. Petr was arrested and then convicted as a spy. He was sentenced to life in prison and forced to share a cell with ISIS terrorists, who didn't take kindly to the Christian missionary.

Petr faced unbearable living conditions for most of his 445 days in prison. Drinking rusty water was just one of the many difficulties he had to deal with on a daily basis. With only one small, dirty blanket, he was forced to sleep on a concrete floor in either ridiculously hot or cold temperatures. Then, as if that wasn't enough, he would be harassed and sometimes physically beaten by his cellmates. Prison officials would even play mind games with him – he would be given the impression that he was going to be released and sent home, only to find out it was a cruel joke.

However, Petr did not break, as many people would have. He had cast his cares to the Lord and put his full trust and faith in Him. Petr eventually got his hands on a Bible, which he read from cover to cover. He found a calling within the bars of the prison, ministering to inmates who were receptive to his messages of the Gospel. Before he knew it, he was actually making an impact with many of his inmates and leading some to Christ.

Friends and family around the world were fasting and praying for him daily. Petr later discussed that during one of his most horrific moments in prison, the elder at his wife's Bible study group had stopped the gathering and asked everyone to get on their knees, pray in earnest for Petr, while declaring victory for the Lord in his prison cell. At this same moment, Petr was on his knees in front of his tormentors being struck repeatedly by a broomstick.

"At the moment I needed prayer maybe more than I have needed it at any other time in my life, the Lord Himself was raising up prayer warriors to battle with me and for me," explained Petr.[8]

During his 14 and a half months in prison, Petr Jasek surrendered completely to the Lord and spent every minute he could sharing the gospel with his fellow prisoners. Today, he serves as Global Ambassador for *Voices of the Martyrs* (VOM) and he travels around the world, telling his story and inspiring many Christians to stand with their suffering brothers and sisters in Christ.

Executed on the Beach

In 2015, the world was horrified to see the images of 21 Coptic Christians kneeling on the beach ready to be executed by Muslim Extremists. Two of the men that fatal day were brothers, so one mother had to witness both of her sons being killed.

How does one withstand that type of grief? This mother knew that this world was not the end and that her sons had stood faithful to the very end. She gave them to God. She cast her sorrow, her anxiety, her anguish to God.

"I thank my God that my two sons did not denounce Jesus; it is an honor and privilege that they died faithful," she proclaimed.

Instead of denouncing their faith in Jesus Christ, the martyrs spoke his name as they were having their throats cut.

"They were ordinary laborers with no theological education, but they were not going to denounce Jesus," Archbishop Mouneer Anis said.[9]

Fortunately, most of us will never be in that horrific situation faced by this Christian mother. However, we all face tribulations of various kinds, and we each have a choice to handle the situations ourselves, to wallow in our misery, or to cast our concerns to the Lord.

Usher Syndrome

Charles Howard Usher was an ophthalmologist from Edinburgh, Scotland who in the early 20th century discovered a connection between deafness and retina pigmentosa. The doctor was able to demonstrate in his findings that the eye disease was inherited and passed on by the parents to their children. He became the namesake of Usher Syndrome, a rare genetic disorder involving hearing loss and this visual impairment.

Usher also had a strong faith in God. At a dire time in his life, his son Frank was very ill. Dr. Usher prayed very hard for his son but to no avail. "I used all the prayer knowledge I possessed on his behalf," explained Usher, "but he continued to worsen. This went on for several weeks."

Charles Usher watched his son lying in bed one day, nearing the end of his life. It was at that moment that the doctor received a flash of wisdom. He cast all his cares -- and his son -- into the Lord's hands. "Oh, God, I have spent much time in prayer for my son, and yet he is no better. I will now leave him to You and give myself to prayer for others. If it is Your will to take him, I choose Your will – I surrender him entirely to You."

He proceeded to call his wife to the room and explain to her what he had done. With tears in her eyes, she joined him in releasing her son to God.

Two days later the Usher's son began to improve, and over the course of a short period, he was completely healed. Charles Usher came to the conclusion that "it was the wrestling of my prayers that had hindered God's answer, and that if I had to continue to wrestle, being unwilling to surrender him to God, he would probably not be here today."[10]

Moving Mountains

Robert G. LeTourneau was a famous industrialist in the early part of the 20th century. He became well known and wealthy by creating earthmoving machinery – equipment that helped build the infrastructure to a young country.[11]

During World War II, LeTourneau was awarded a contract with the U.S. government to develop large machinery to lift airplanes. No machine of this complicated nature had ever been designed before.

It wasn't long before LeTourneau and his team of engineers were at a loss. They simply did not know how it could be done. So much was at stake. While frustrated and under a tight deadline,

LeTourneau finally told his team, "Well, boys, I'm knocking off. I'm going to a prayer meeting."

"Why, you can't do that boss," a member of his team stated emphatically. "We have got a deadline on this thing."

LeTourneau explained to his team that he had a deadline with God, instead. He went to the prayer meeting and cast his cares to the One who could solve the problem. He prayed, sung old hymns and put himself into complete harmony with his maker.

After the meeting, LeTourneau was walking along the street when the complete design that he and his team was seeking popped into his head. He returned to his team of engineers with the design God had given him – the first machine of its kind.

Robert LeTourneau knew Who to turn to when he was facing an obstacle. During his amazing career in which he secured over 300 patents, LeTourneau's name became synonymous with earth-moving machinery. It is estimated that nearly 70 percent of the earthmoving equipment and vehicles employed by the Allies in World War II came from his factories. Today, a Christian-based polytechnic university in Longview, Texas, bears his name.

The Truth

"No one in the world can change Truth. What we can do and should do is to seek truth and to serve it when we have found it. The real conflict is the inner conflict. Beyond armies of occupation and the hecatombs of extermination camps, there are two irreconcilable enemies in the depth of every soul: good and evil, sin and love. And what use are the victories on the battlefield if we ourselves are defeated in our innermost personal selves?" ~ St. Maximilian Kolbe, martyr at the hands of the Nazis

Maximillian Kolbe was a priest who was an outspoken critic of the Third Reich. In 1939 around the start of the Second World War, Kolbe was arrested under general suspicion but later released. Two years later, he was arrested again for hiding and protecting Jewish people. This time there would be no release. He was sent to the Auschwitz concentration camp to do hard labor.

At Auschwitz the priest was singled out by a vicious and cruel guard who would make Kolbe perform the hardest tasks and also beat him savagely. In the face of this evil behavior, Kolbe remained calm and at peace with complete confidence in God.

In the summer of 1941, several months after Kolbe entered Auschwitz, three prisoners escaped from the concentration camp. The remaining prisoners would have to pay for this deed. As punishment for the escape, the Deputy Commander ordered 10 men to be placed in an underground bunker where they would starve to death. A prisoner, Franciszek Gajowniczek, was one of the men chosen.

When Kolbe heard Gajowniczek cry out, "My wife! My children!" Kolbe volunteered to take his place. Amazed by this act, the Nazi guards allowed the priest to take his place.[12]

Franciszek Gajowniczek would miraculously survive Auschwitz. He would later be present at the ceremony when Kolbe was canonized as a saint by the Roman Catholic Church in 1971.

Kolbe continued to minister and serve the prisoners with whom he was sharing this awful circumstance. He sat in the underground cell, starving to death and waiting to die, but he was at complete peace. How is that possible? Over his lifetime Maximillian Kolbe had developed complete faith and trust in his Maker, and he had learned to cast all his cares to Him.

Action Item

Choose one of these amazing stories to inspire you.

At the appropriate times, re-tell the story to family, friends and those who need encouragement.

Chapter Fourteen
The Creator – Evidence

"**Where were you when I laid the earth's foundation?** Tell me, if you understand. Who marked off its dimensions? Surely you know! Who stretched a measuring line across it? On what were its footings set, or who laid its cornerstone—while the morning stars sang together and all the angels shouted for joy?"
~ Job 38:4-7 (NIV)

How does one begin to write and correctly convey the majesty of the Creator of the universe? I found this a very arduous task, so I humbly present the following attempt.

In the summer of 2022, NASA released photos from the James Webb Telescope, the largest telescope ever built. The photos went well beyond what you saw from the Hubble Telescope back in the early 1990s. What the public saw from the Webb telescope were pictures with more clarity than ever before seen from space.

Pillars of the Earth

The incredible Pillars of the Earth photo[1] from 1995 seemed like it could never be topped in our lifetime...until now. The Webb telescope delivers the deepest and sharpest infrared image of the distant universe ever seen. By bringing distant galaxies into sharp focus, this technological advancement allows one to observe 48 individual galaxies at the same time. What looks like an image of stars is actually the galaxy cluster SMACS 0723. Each star-like image is an entire galaxy. Incredible, and in many ways, hard to fully comprehend.

"There's so much going on here, it's so beautiful," said Amber Straughn, an astrophysicist at NASA's Goddard Space Flight Center in Maryland. "Today, for the first time, we're seeing brand new stars that were previously completely hidden from our view."[2]

"The exact blueprints for the development of life are not yet known." ~ Center for Astrophysics, Harvard & Smithsonian – August, 2022.[3]

In his book Miracles, Eric Metaxas summarizes all the different, amazing aspects of God and His creation. He explains how the probability of life on earth is so minuscule that it defies logic. When scientist Carl Sagan and other colleagues first commented on what conditions were required to support life on a planet, they believed that there were only two requirements. Decades later, those conditions have risen to over 150.[4]

One of the most fascinating conditions for life involves our moon. The earth is the only planet in our solar system with only one moon. What if earth had two moons? First, the two moons would work against each other, resulting in a gravitational pull back and forth, causing all sorts of problems on the surfaces of both moons.[5] The presence of two moons would result in peak tidal pulls on earth's oceans six times greater than current conditions. Many of our greatest cities, which are in close proximity to oceans, would cease to exist. Life would be a lot different, if it would exist at all.

Fortunately, though, there is one moon that resides in the perfect proximity from the earth and it plays a pivotal role to life on the planet. Its affect on time, tides, and light plays essential roles in the lives of every living creature on our planet. Earth's current length of day, stable seasons, and tides are all determined by the moon's gravitational pull.

The moon-earth relationship works because of the size of the moon relative to earth and the distance between them. If the moon was significantly larger, for example, its pull on the tides would cause devastation across the continents.

The earth has its seasons because of its tilt and rotational axis. The moon actually works as a stabilizer for the earth's tilt, so again the distance between the two is just right to make everything work. Move the moon a different distance between it and earth, and everything changes. Life ceases to exist as you know it.

"The moon stabilizes Earth's orbit and keeps its conditions stable," explains Professor Sabine Stanley. "Without the Earth-Moon system, the Earth would even face radical climate changes every few hundred years. Thus, life would have probably been significantly changed, if not destroyed."[6]

The moon has an effect on life here on earth in more ways than you can possibly imagine. Just take the situation with the coral reef in Australia. There is an annual event at the Great Barrier Reef every November following the full moon. Every November, a few days after the full moon, there is a mass coral spawning.[7] Scientists don't fully understand why this happens, but they believe that the period of darkness between sunset and moonrise triggers synchronized mass spawning and leads to the expansion of life in the coral reef. Bottom line, the moon has a massive effect on life in the Southern Hemisphere's coral reef.

The sun, of course, has its own gravitational pull on the earth and its oceans. The three – sun, earth, moon – work in concert together and create the conditions for life on this planet. Alter the size of the moon or sun, or the distance between the three, and everything changes in a bad way. It's highly doubtful that life would exist on earth if any of these factors were altered by the slightest of percentages.

Dr. James P. Gills who founded St. Luke's Cataract and Laser Institute in my town of Tarpon Springs, Florida, is considered by many to be the top cataract surgeon in the world. In addition to restoring physical vision, he has dedicated his life to helping people gain a clear spiritual vision.

Dr. Gills was not always such a strong believer in the faith. However, when he was a young medical student, it was the study of the human cell that really transformed his perspective on God and His incredible design. Upon taking a deep dive into the study and examination of one human cell, Dr. Gills came to the conclusion that it could not be explained. He had attempted to write a book on the subject but quickly came to the conclusion that he lacked the knowledge and understanding of how a single cell functioned.

Realizing that not even the most brilliant scientists in the world understood how a human cell functioned within the body, Dr. Gills was drawn closer to God.

"You and I are God's most prized creation; we are a miracle of design," said Dr. Gills. "Were we to see ourselves as such in the mirror every morning, and we were to give honest attention to the unfathomable mysteries of our cells and their seamless integration into our body, we would immediately understand that our Creator is beautiful and sovereign. We would raise our arms in the joy of life and appreciation for our lord. We would put under our feet the desire to be independent of Him or defy Him. We would walk at His side throughout the day."[8]

John Henry Jowett, British preacher and author, stated, "The ability of God is beyond our prayers, beyond our largest prayers. I have been thinking of some of the petitions that have entered into my supplication innumerable times. What have I asked for? I have asked for a cupful, and the ocean remains. I have asked for a sunbeam, and the sun abides. My best asking falls immeasurably short of my Father's giving; it is beyond what we can ask."[9]

Many people want to fully understand God and put Him in a box. For those of you who are parents, do you expect your children to understand everything that you as an adult comprehends? Of course not. Just as the difference between adults and children is immense, the difference in the knowledge between humans and God is incalculable. God is way bigger than we even realize, and his power to work miracles in our lives is more do-able than we can possibly imagine. He can handle whatever you throw at him.

So why are you holding back from the Creator of the universe? God is way bigger and more powerful than human minds can comprehend. When you really start to think about that fact, you realize how tiny your prayers have been. Don't let your prayers be limited to an earthly mindset.

The same God who hung the sun, moon, planets, and stars, and who holds all of time and space in His hands, hears your prayers. Can He not handle the minuscule problems that you cast to Him?

Isaiah 55:9 says, "For as the heavens are higher than the earth, so are My ways higher than your ways, and My thoughts than your thoughts."[10]

He knows better than you. He knows better than me. He can handle whatever you throw at him. In confidence and complete trust, cast your cares to the Creator of the universe. Then, sit back and enjoy the peace that transcends all understanding. God bless!

Addendum

21 Days of Verses to Memorize

Take the next three weeks and memorize one verse per day. Recite it to yourself several times throughout the day until it is seared into your memory.

Day One

Rejoice always, pray without ceasing, give thanks in all circumstances; for this is the will of God in Christ Jesus for you.

1 Thessalonians 5:16-18 (ESV)

Day Two

For God has not given us a spirit of fear, but of power and of love and of a sound mind.

2 Timothy 1:7 (NKJV)

Day Three

But seek first his kingdom and his righteousness, and all these things will be given to you as well.

Matthew 6:33 (NIV)

Day Four

Let us not become weary in doing good, for at the proper time we will reap a harvest if we do not give up.

Galatians 6:9 (NIV)

Day Five

Good sense makes one slow to anger, and it is his glory to overlook an offense.

Proverbs 19:11 (ESV)

Day Six

Set a guard over my mouth, LORD; keep watch over the door of my lips.

Psalm 141:3 (NIV)

Day Seven

Let the word of Christ dwell in you richly...

Colossians 3:16 (ESV)

Day Eight

No foul language should come from your mouth, but only what is good for building up someone in need, so that it gives grace to those who hear.

Ephesians 4:29 (CSB)

Day Nine

Do not let this book of the law depart from your lips. Recite it by day and by night, that you may carefully observe all that is written in it; then you will attain your goal; then you will succeed.

Joshua 1:8 (NAB)

Day 10

Blessed is the man who endures temptation; for when he has been approved, he will receive the crown of life which the Lord has promised to those who love Him.

James 1:12 (NKJV)

Day 11

Do not merely listen to the Word, and so deceive yourselves. Do what it says.

James 1:22 (NIV)

Day 12

For we are God's handiwork, created in Christ Jesus to do good works, which God prepared in advance for us to do.

Ephesians 2:10 (NIV)

Day 13

In him lie hidden all the treasures of wisdom and knowledge.

Colossians 2:3 (NLT)

Day 14

When I am afraid, I put my trust in you. In God, whose word I praise — in God I trust and am not afraid. What can mere mortals do to me?

Psalm 56:3-4 (NIV)

Day 15

The fear of the Lord is the beginning of wisdom; all those who practice it have a good understanding. His praise endures forever!

Psalm 111:10 (ESV)

Day 16

Have nothing to do with foolish, ignorant controversies; you know that they breed quarrels.

2 Timothy 2:23 (ESV)

Day 17

My dear brothers and sisters, take note of this: Everyone should be quick to listen, slow to speak and slow to become angry, because human anger does not produce the righteousness that God desires.

James 1:19-20 (NIV)

Day 18

As each has received a gift, use it to serve one another, as good stewards of God's varied grace: whoever speaks, as one who speaks oracles of God; whoever serves, as one who serves by the strength that God supplies—in order that in everything God may be glorified through Jesus Christ. To him belong glory and dominion forever and ever. Amen.

1 Peter 4:10-11 (ESV)

Day 19

Always be full of joy in the Lord. I say it again — rejoice!

Philippians 4:4 (NLT)

Day 20

You will keep in perfect peace all who trust in you, all whose thoughts are fixed on you!

Isaiah 26:3 (NLT)

Day 21

But the Lord is faithful, and He will strengthen you and protect you from the evil one.

2 Thessalonians 3:3 (NIV)

Addendum 2

Select Verses about Casting Your Cares onto the Lord

"Cast your burden on the LORD, and he will sustain you; he will never permit the righteous to be moved." ~ Psalm 55:22 (ESV)

"Commit your way to the LORD; trust in him, and he will act." ~ Psalm 37:5 (ESV)

"Be still before the Lord and wait patiently for him; do not fret when people succeed in their ways, when they carry out their wicked schemes." ~ Psalm 37:7 (NIV)

"When I am afraid, I put my trust in you. In God, whose word I praise, in God I trust; I shall not be afraid. What can flesh do to me?" ~ Psalm 56:3-4 (ESV)

"I sought the Lord and He answered. He delivered me from all my fears." ~ Psalm 34: 4 (ESV)

"The eyes of the LORD are toward the righteous and his ears toward their cry." ~ Psalm 34:15 (ESV)

"I believe that I shall look upon the goodness of the LORD in the land of the living! Wait for the LORD; be strong, and let your heart take courage; wait for the LORD!" ~ Psalm 27:13-14 (ESV)

"Be still and know that I am God." ~ Psalm 46:10 (ESV)

"Then call on me when you are in trouble, and I will rescue you and you will give me glory." ~ Psalm 50:15 (NLT)

"Praise be to the Lord, to God our Savior, who daily bears our burdens." ~ Psalm 68:19 (NIV)

"Listen to me, O house of Jacob, all you who remain of the house of Israel, you whom I have upheld since you were conceived, and have carried since your birth. Even to your old age and gray hairs I am he, I am he who will sustain you. I have made you and I will carry you; I will sustain you and I will rescue you." ~ Isaiah 46:4 (NIV)

"The Lord your God is with you, He is might to save." ~ Zephaniah 3:17 (BSB)

"Everyone who calls on the name of the Lord will be saved." ~ Joel 2:32 (ESV)

"Look to the right and see: there is none who takes notice of me; no refuge remains to me; no one cares for my soul. I cry to you, O LORD; I say, You are my refuge, my portion in the land of the living." ~ Psalm 142:4-5 (ESV)

"And David was greatly distressed, for the people spoke of stoning him, because all the people were bitter in soul, each for his sons and daughters. But David strengthened himself in the LORD his God." ~ 1 Samuel 30:6 (ESV)

New Testament

"Do not be anxious about anything, but in everything by prayer and supplication with thanksgiving let your requests be made known to God." ~ Philippians 4:13 (ESV)

"Therefore I tell you, do not be anxious about your life, what you will eat or what you will drink, nor about your body, what you will put on. Is not life more than food, and the body more than clothing? Look at the birds of the air: they neither sow nor reap nor gather into barns, and yet your heavenly Father feeds them. Are you not of more value than they?" ~ Matthew 6:25-26 (ESV)

"But seek first the kingdom of God and his righteousness, and all these things will be added to you. Therefore do not be anxious about tomorrow, for tomorrow will be anxious for itself. Sufficient for the day is its own trouble." ~ Matthew 6:33-34 (ESV)

And he said to his disciples, "Therefore I tell you, do not be anxious about your life, what you will eat, nor about your body, what you will put on." ~ Luke 12:22 (ESV)

"Keep your life free from love of money, and be content with what you have, for he has said, 'I will never leave you nor forsake you.' So, we can confidently say, 'The Lord is my helper; I will not fear; what can man do to me?'" ~ Hebrews 13:5-6 (ESV)

"For all the nations of the world seek after these things, and your Father knows that you need them. Instead, seek his kingdom, and these things will be added to you. Fear not, little flock, for it is your Father's good pleasure to give you the kingdom." ~ Luke 12:30-32 (ESV)

"And when they bring you before the synagogues and the rulers and the authorities, do not be anxious about how you should defend yourself or what you should say, for the Holy Spirit will teach you in that very hour what you ought to say." ~ Luke 12:11-12 (ESV)

"If any of you lacks wisdom, you should ask God, who gives generously to all without finding fault, and it will be given to you. But when you ask, you must believe and not doubt, because the one who doubts is like a wave of the sea, blown and tossed by the wind." ~ James 1:5 (NIV)

"'Have faith in God,' Jesus answered [the disciples]. 'Truly I tell you, if anyone says to this mountain, 'Go, throw yourself into the sea,' and does not doubt in their heart but believes that what they say will happen, it will be done for them. Therefore I tell you, whatever you ask for in prayer, believe that you have received it, and it will be yours. And when you stand praying, if you hold anything against anyone, forgive them, so that your Father in heaven may forgive you your sins.'" Mark 11:22-26 (NIV)

"For God has not given you a spirit of fear, but of power, love, and self-control." ~ 2 Timothy 1:7 (BSB)

Scriptures of God's Promises

"In your strength I can crush an army; with my God I can scale any wall. God's way is perfect. All the Lord's promises are true. He is a shield for all who look to him for protection." ~ Psalm 18:29-30 (NIV)

"I will strengthen you and help you; I will uphold you with my righteous right hand." ~ Isaiah 41:10 (NIV)

"Fear not [Richard], for I have redeemed you; I have called you by name, you are mine." ~ Isaiah 43:1 (ESV)

"The Lord is good, a strong refuge when trouble comes. He is close to those who trust in Him." ~ Nahum 1:7 (NLT)

"No one will be able to stand against you all the days of your life. As I was with Moses, so I will be with you; I will never leave you nor forsake you." ~ Joshua 1:5 (NIV)

"Then you will call upon me and come and pray to me, and I will hear you. You will seek me and find me, when you seek me with all your heart." ~ Jeremiah 29:12-13 (ESV)

"Submit to God and be at peace with him; in this way prosperity will come to you." ~ Job 22:21 (NIV)

Acknowledgments

My faith journey began at a young age thanks to my late parents, MaryAnn and Richard Nilsen, who were married an amazing 62 years. They provided me a strong foundation in the Lord. Thank you to them and all of my siblings who have provided love and guidance throughout my life.

Thank you to my best friend and partner in life, Marta, who has provided me invaluable support over these past many years. She is an amazing mother to our three beautiful daughters – Natalie, Genesis and Paradise – each of whom have supported me in their own way during the writing process.

A special thank you goes out to Sammy Schafer who provided not only excellent editing advice but vital insight into telling the stories within CAST. Thank you to editor Shannon Gale who caught several mistakes within these writings. I am grateful to both of my editors for their contributions.

Thank you to my friends who took the time to read CAST and provide their feedback: Denise Crompton, Dan Miller, Christina Blackmon, Michael Allen, Cindy Fay, Sheryl Crosier and Nina Carothers.

Finally, I want to thank you for reading my book and for sharing it with friends and family who are going through life's struggles. My prayer is that you and your loved ones will give your troubles to God and let Him provide the solutions.

SHARE CAST WITH YOUR FRIENDS AND FAMILY

If this book helped you, then please consider spreading the word. You can take a few minutes to write a positive review on the site where you purchased this book.

If you have a blog, you could write a short book review on your site and share this powerful message.

For those of you with Facebook, Instagram, Pinterest, X/Twitter, or other social-networking accounts, feel free to share information about this book with your friends and fans.

If you are in a small group, please share with your friends.

Thank you for your purchase of CAST: 1 Peter 5:7.

Thank you and God bless.

About the Author

Richard Nilsen resides with his wife of nearly 25 years, Marta, and their three beautiful daughters in historic Tarpon Springs, Florida. He and his wife were foster parents for several years prior to adopting their two youngest daughters.

Nilsen is the founder of All Star Press, a book publishing and marketing firm.

Also By Richard Nilsen

The Road to Recovery (e-book)

Sleep Great for Life (available in print and e-book)

Secrets to a Great Vacation: Glacier National Park (e-book)

Other Publications from All Star Press -

Books That Change Lives

"I Am Not a Syndrome - My Name is Simon" by Sheryl Crosier

"Diagnosis: Rare Disease" by Denise Crompton

"The Imposter Nurse" by Denise Crompton (e-book)

"Angel Gabriel – a True Story" by Joy LaPlante (e-book)

The Color Olors childrens' book series by Nina L. Carothers

"Goodnight, Boone" children's book by Yogi Collins

"Quiet Spaces: Hearing God's Call in a Noisy World" by James Hale (e-book)

"Getting Seen: Ultimate Resume Guide" By James Hale (e-book)

"My Wild Ride: The Untamed Life of a Girl with No Self-esteem" by Susan Bump

"The House That Richard Built: Life Lessons as a Carpenter's Son" by James D. Smith (e-book)

References

CHAPTER 1: He Lived Among ISIS Yet Slept in Peace

1. Petr Jasek, *Imprisoned with ISIS*, (Washington, D.C.: Salem Books, 2020).

CHAPTER 2: Definition of Casting

1. Jason Sealock, *8 Factors That Affect Casting Distance*, May 15, 2014, (https://www.wired2fish.com/bass-fishing/8-factors-that-affect-casting-distance/).

CHAPTER 3: Our Will Be Done

1. Exodus 2:11-15 (NIV).

2. Exodus 4:1 (BSB).

3. Exodus 4:10 (BSB).

4. Exodus 14: 11-12 (NIV).

5. Exodus 14: 13 (NIV).

6. Exodus 14: 19-31 (NIV).

CHAPTER 4: Faith in Action

1. Public domain, *Lincoln - The Political Blondin*, (Harper's Weekly 1 Sep 1864.jpg).

2. Biography.com, Hernan Cortes, April 2, 2014, (https://www.biography.com/explorer/hernan-cortes)

3. Warner Bros., John Fogarty, *Centerfield* (January, 1985).

4. James 2:17 (BSB).

CHAPTER 5: How to Cast Our Cares to the Lord

1. 1 Peter 2:9 (ESV).

2. Mark 11:23 (NIV).

3. Norman Vincent Peale, *Enthusiasm Makes the Difference*, (New York: Foundation for Christian Living, 1967), 235.

4. James 1:6 (NIV).

5. Numbers 13: 27-33 (NIV).

6. L. B. Cowman, *Streams in the Desert* (Grand Rapids: Zondervan, 1997), 127.

7. John 11:41-42 (ESV).

8. Luke 10:41-42 (NIV).

9. Matthew 22:29 (ESV).

10. Author, *One-Minute Insights for Men*, (Eugene: Harvest House Publishers, 2013).

11. C.S. Lewis, A Letter to Mrs. L.

12. A.W. Tozer, *The Counselor*, (Chicago: Moody Publishers, 1993), 144.

13. *The Wisdom of Fulton Sheen* (North Palm Beach: Blue Sparrow, 2021), 18.

14. Philippians 4:8 (NIV).

CHAPTER 6: Biblical Guidance for Casting Our Cares to God

1. John 3:16 (NIV).

2. *Tim Tebow Rules*, ESPN, Feb. 14, 2010, (https://www.espn.com/blog/sportscenter/post/_/id/31088/tim-tebow-rules-according-to-the-ncaa).

3. Philippians 4:13 (NKJV).

4. 1 Peter 5:2 (NIV).

5. 1 Peter 5:2-3 (NIV).

6. 1 Peter 5:5-6 (NIV).

7. *A Message from Bishop Michael F. Burbidge*, Arlington Diocese.org, Easter 2021.

8. Psalm 86:1 (NIV).

9. *Social media use and depression in adolescents: a scoping review*, National Library of Medicine, July 30, 2020, (https://www.ncbi.nlm.nih.gov/pmc/articles/PMC7392374/).

10. Philippians 4:8 (NIV).

CHAPTER 8: Control Your Intake

1. Ephesians 4:29 (NIV).

2. Proverbs 12:25 (HCSB).

CHAPTER 9: The Freedom of the Son

1. Luke 15:11-32 (ESV).

CHAPTER 10: Some of Our Cares?

1. Proverbs 3:5-6 (NIV).

CHAPTER 11: His Eyes Are on the Sparrow

1. *History of Hymns: "His Eye Is on the Sparrow,"* Discipleship Ministries, June, 2013, (https://www.umcdiscipleship.org/resources/history-of-hymns-his-eye-is-on-the-sparrow).

CHAPTER 12: A Treasure Trove of Blessings

1. 1 Samuel 17:4-58 (NAB).

CHAPTER 13: Real World Examples

1. Interview on Youtube, (https://youtu.be/C8Ys2fa7jZk).

2. *It Is Well With My Soul,* lyrics © Bethel Music Publishing, Capitol CMG Publishing, Integrity Music, Universal Music Publishing Group, Walt Disney Music Company, Warner Chappell Music, Inc. Songwriters: Christopher C. C. Stafford / Philip Paul Bliss.

3. Kaleigh McEnany, *For Such a Time As This*, (New York: Post Hill Press, 2021), 201.

4. Kaleigh McEnany, *For Such a Time As This*, (New York: Post Hill Press, 2021), 203.

5. (https://en.wikipedia.org/wiki/Siloam_inscription, http://cojs.org/hezekiah-s_-or_siloam-_tunnel_inscripti

on-_701_bce/).

6. Christopher Rollston, *The Siloam Inscription and Hezekiah's Tunnel*, Bible Odyssey (https://www.bibleodyssey.org/places/related-articles/the-siloam-inscription-and-hezekiahs-tunnel/).

7. Benjamin Weinthal, *Biblical site where Jesus healed blind man excavated for public view: Affirms Scripture*, January 2, 2023, (https://nypost.com/2023/01/02/biblical-site-where-jesus-healed-blind-man-excavated-for-public-view-affirms-scripture/)

8. Petr Jasek, *Imprisoned with ISIS*, (Washington, D.C. : Salem Books, 2020), pg. 212-3.

9. David W. Virtue, *CAIRO: Mother proud of her two sons who did not renounce Jesus as they were beheaded by ISIS*, Virtueonline.org, October 5, 2016, (https://virtueonline.org/cairo-mother-proud-her-two-sons-who-did-not-renounce-jesus-they-were-beheaded-isis).

10. L. B. Cowman, *Streams in the Desert* (Grand Rapids: Zondervan, 1997).

11. Norman Vincent Peale, *How To Handle Tough Times*, (New York: Peale Center For Christian Living, 1990).

12. *Biography of Saint Maximilian Kolbe*, Saint Maximilian Kolbe Church, (https://www.stmaximiliankolbechurch.com/about-us/biography-of-saint-maximilian).

CHAPTER 14: The Creator – Evidence

1. Eagle Nebula Pillars, Wiki Commons, (https://commons.wikimedia.org/wiki/File:Eagle_nebula_pillars.jpg).

2. Megan Bartles, *Gallery: James Webb Space Telescope's 1st Photos*, July 15, 2022, (https://www.space.com/james-webb-space-telescope-first-photos).

3. *What Conditions Are Necessary For Life*, Center for Astrophysics, August 2022, (https://www.cfa.harvard.edu/big-questions/what-conditions-are-necessary-life).

4. Eric Metaxas, *Miracles*, (New York: Dutton, 2014), 36.

5. Gina Echevarria and Shira Polan, *What would happen if Earth had 2 moons*, Jan 10, 2019, (https://www.businessinsider.com/what-if-earth-had-two-moons-tides-sea-level-collision-2019-1).

6. Sabine Stanley, *The Past and the Future of the Earth-Moon System*, John Hopkins University, July 15, 2020, (https://www.wondriumdaily.com/the-past-and-the-future-of-the-earth-moon-system/).

7. *Moonrise timing is key for synchronized spawning in coral - Dipsastraea speciosa*, Pnas.org, August 9, 2021, (https://www.pnas.org/doi/10.1073/pnas.2101985118).

8. James P. Gills MD, *Overcoming Spiritual Blindness*, (Lake Mary: Creation House, 2005), 97.

9. L. B. Cowman, *Streams in the Desert* (Grand Rapids: Zondervan, 1997), 289.

10. Isaiah 55:9 (NIV).